Advance Praise For Accountants! *Go Narrow*

I think the future of accounting firms is away from generalists and toward specialized niches. Read this book, "Accountants! *Go Narrow*" and learn how your career as an accountant or as the managing partner of an accounting firm can get focused to achieve the success you've dreamed about. Alice presents a compelling proposition that industry specialization is not only a differentiator, but also the roadmap to get focused on growth and enhanced client experience, which will be a game changer for your firm and your talented professionals. The inspiring stories from the firms Alice helped, from very large to much smaller, are scalable for firms of every size and accountants at any stage of their careers. Read it and you will have a vision of a successful and satisfying accounting career at a firm managed to support that focused career growth.

Mike Maksymiw, Jr., CPA, CGMA,
Executive Director of Aprio Firm Alliance

Awesome is the word. Alice Lerman delivers a dynamic, high-impact, and inspiring message in "Accountants! *Go Narrow*". She motivates and empowers your professionals to become industry thought leaders to grow their careers and the firm. This is a must-have book for your management team and your firm's professionals.

Samantha Inczauskis MBA,
Senior Industry Project Manager, Marcum LLP

Alice's expertise and experience empowers her to help firm managing partners and industry practice group leaders make more money by going narrow. Having led all aspects of industry programs at a Big Four firm and three other top 20 CPA firms, I'm confident that Alice will be a great industry strategy advisor to coach your firm too.

Allan D. Koltin, CPA, CGMACEO,
Koltin Consulting Group, Inc

Alice is a powerful leader and brilliant teacher who ignites the best in others. Her book, "Accountants! *Go Narrow*" is a must read for accountants striving to differentiate themselves from the competition in a crowded marketplace. Now is the time for you to get focused and harness the power of industry specialization for your career and your firm. Alice will help you get to your goal.

Carrie Sechel, retired Partner at Deloitte Tax,
former Chief of Staff to the Deloitte US Real Estate Leader,
and bestselling author of BASE Jump

The book in your hands will empower you to transform your firm or jumpstart your own career by Going Narrow. Alice will inspire you and the professionals in your firm, across Assurance, Tax and Advisory, to get focused on a narrow target market. She provides the secret sauce used by successful firms. Alice inspires and coaches young professionals starting out, through industry practice leaders, to engage with clients by going deep in the client's world — their business and their industry. I've had the privilege of working with Alice for many years, where she led transformative industry-focused programs at RSM to elevate and provide competitive differentiation to enhance value to clients and assist people go from good to great.

> Gary Sturisky, CPA, Former Managing Partner RSM Consulting, author of Crunch Time: CPA Firm Survival in a Predatory Environment

When Alice joined our team she brought a whole new perspective on the value and strength that industry focus can bring to a firm. Alice implemented new ideas and strategies to create effective programs across the board. Alice spent time with industry leaders to strategize and create actionable steps that built a stronger team and delivered measurable results. As someone with great knowledge, and a deep understanding of the accounting industry and the industries we serve, Alice leads the way when it comes to building collaborative teams and assisting in building a cohesive brand for the industry groups.

> Joe Natarelli, CPA, Partner and National Construction Industry Leader, Marcum

I worked with Alice Lerman for over six years. During this time, she took RSM's National Industry Program from infancy to strength and maturity. She demonstrates inspiring leadership by blending analytical thinking with creative ideas, and then executes via collaboration with upper management and a wide array of professionals. Alice built a cohesive high-performing team to define and execute a strategic vision with perseverance and dedication to delivery excellence. She has drive, passion and lots of energy.

Mendy Nudelman, Retired Partner and National Industry Leader at RSM/McGladrey

"Accountants! *Go Narrow!*" is an extraordinary book filled with wisdom and practices to design an accountant's successful career, and an accounting firm's roadmap to achieve financial success. I've had the great fortune of knowing Alice Lerman as a mentor and career coach, and she is a remarkable, engaging, and gifted leader. She has created one of the most powerful coaching tools to help accounting firms build an industry specialization strategy that will accelerate revenue growth AND attract and retain talent for your firm.

Todj Gozdeck, CPA, Transaction Advisory Services and Private Equity Partner at Marcum.

I have had the pleasure of working with Alice at two firms — RSM (McGladrey) and Deloitte. She is, without a doubt, one of the most well-versed industry professionals I've worked with. She was instrumental in helping RSM establish and build its industry market focus and has continued to provide critical input as the firm increases its focus on key industries. She is insightful, thoughtful, and candid when needed. I always found it refreshing to discuss problems with her, as she was able to point out areas to focus on and suggest viable solutions. She is an asset to any organization lucky enough to engage with her.

Sean Fox, Senior Managing Consultant at IBM

Accountants! *Go Narrow*

Accountants!
Go Narrow

**Turn the Power of
Industry Specialization into
Profit for Your Firm**

*An insider's guide to building an industry
specialization strategy for
your CPA/consulting firm*

Alice Lerman, JD, MBA

Accountants! *Go Narrow*
Turn the Power of Industry Specialization into Profit for Your Firm
An insider's guide to building an industry specialization strategy for your CPA/consulting firm

By Alice Lerman, JD, MBA

Published by:
Jomase Publishers
1-201-639-8860
www.lermanstrategies.com

Cover Design and Interior Design by Arrow North, LLC

ISBN: 979-8-218-03987-5

This book does not contain any legal advice. Author and publisher disclaim and all warranties, losses, costs, claims, demands, suits or accident of any type or nature whatsoever, arising from, or in any related to this book, the use of this book, and/or claims that a particular technique or device in this book is legal or reasonable in any jurisdiction.

© Copyright 2022 by Jomase Publishing

All rights reserved. No part of this book may be reproduced or transmitted in any form or by any means, electronic or mechanical, including photographing, recording or by any information storage or retrieval system, without written permission from the author, except for the inclusion of brief quotations in a review.

First Edition, 2022
Published in the United States of America

Making contact with the author for speaking, coaching or consulting or ordering large book quantities is hassle free.
Simply reach out to Alice at alice@lermanstrategies.com.

*For my sister, Dr. Ethel Lippman,
who has inspired my journey.
And is the best sister a woman could ask for.*

*And to my husband, Jim,
who walks with me every step of the way.*

No one achieves greatness by becoming a generalist.

–John C. Maxwell

Table of Contents

Introduction: 1
What Industry Specialization Is About and What It Is *Not*

1. Greatness Isn't Achieved by Generalists 4
Industry specialization can work for your firm and your firm's professionals. People are your firm's most important asset. Industry knowledge and expertise raises the intellectual capital bar and differentiates your firm in the marketplace.

REALITY CHECK
Strategies for supporting industry groups with limited resources.

2. Your Industry Program's Value Proposition 13
Industry knowledge and experience command higher prices in the marketplace and deliver greater value to clients.

REALITY CHECK
The real estate industry practice at RSM exemplified how focusing on the client, in the context of deep industry expertise, is a differentiator that leads to winning in the marketplace.

3. Walk a Mile in Your Clients' Shoes **23**
Generic technical expertise isn't enough. Clients want service providers who know their industry.

REALITY CHECK
Categorizing or mapping prospects, clients and revenues to specific industries can be tricky.

4. Specialties and "Client Experience Excellence" Growth Strategies **30**
CPA/professional services firms on sustainable growth trajectories specialize in chosen industries. Industry specialization is also the path to career success for your firm's people.

REALITY CHECK
Handling power struggles.

5. Why You Need Effective Industry Teams and How to Get There **39**
Industry teams are the essential building blocks of your firm – all you need is a plan.

REALITY CHECK
To meet or not to meet?

6. It's All About Establishing a Growth Mindset **48**

Everyone in the firm must develop a growth mindset that recognizes the critical importance of industry to your firm and its clients.

REALITY CHECK
Industry leaders are groomed – not born.

7. Coaching Your People through the Industry Specialization Process **62**

Becoming a firm/professional with known industry specialties is a multifaceted process. Establish a strong foundation and build from there.

REALITY CHECK
A knowledge management program and the right technology are the keys to effectively sharing your firm's assets and capabilities.

8. Think of Each Industry as a Close-knit Community **76**

Viewing industries as close-knit communities makes it easy to find direction and focus when building industry networks and reputations as industry specialists.

REALITY CHECK
Marketing is a profession too!

9. An Outstanding Client Experience Drives the Firm of the Future 84

Defining your firm's client experience and delivering it consistently across the firm is a golden ticket to becoming a true Firm of the Future.

REALITY CHECK
Building trust between partners and encouraging "firm-first" and "client-first" behaviors can supercharge growth.

---

10. Industry Program + Client Experience Strategy = Accelerated Growth 97

What do clients think of when they think of your firm? Your professionals? Have you clearly articulated the firm's "sweet spot" target market? Why your industry program must operate in lockstep with an outstanding client experience.

REALITY CHECK
Industry vs. sector, or "A rose by any other name would smell as sweet."

---

11. Become a Recognized Industry Luminary 108

As your firm and your people become recognized industry thought leaders, business owners and managers in those industries will begin looking to your firm for help in achieving their business goals.

REALITY CHECK
Be a blowfish and use the game-changer strategy.

12. Get Going! **115**

Most likely, your firm has enough industry expertise to begin your program immediately. You undoubtedly have pockets of industry expertise ready to be more fully leveraged. The first step is recognizing the need and how advantageous an industry program can be for your firm's financial health and sustainability.

APPENDIXES

Appendix I: **119**
Ten Steps to Executing the Successful Industry Strategy

Appendix II: **124**
A Phased Approach to Building an Industry Specialization Strategy

Appendix III: **131**
Sample Client Experience Standards, Based on Client/Prospect Tiers

Glossary **132**

Introduction:

What Industry Specialization Is About and What It Is *Not*

Accountants! *Go Narrow* focuses on the power of industry specialization and on helping professionals develop the business acumen to become better business advisors to clients in their chosen industries. The content is not geared to technical areas of service expertise, which can be acquired through professional accounting associations such as the American Institute of Certified Public Accountants (AICPA).

For Your Firm
For sustainable growth, you want your firm to be the preferred "trusted advisor" for your clients. Being a trusted advisor with the ability to guide clients through their business challenges requires deep industry expertise that's recognized in the markets you serve. That industry experience and knowledge must be embedded in how you serve your clients and face the marketplace.

For Your People
Specialization is the road to career success for almost every accounting professional. While niche expertise in a service line is one route to specialization, the focus of this guidebook is on specialization in a chosen industry. This industry

specialization road map to career success has been my focus as an advisor to accounting and consulting firm management and as a career coach for their professionals. This should also be the focus for you and most of your firm's professionals.

While there are many industries and sectors to consider as you decide what your firm's specialties will be, building that industry depth and expertise follows the same model and process applied across industries. This guidebook provides a universally successful method, a step-by-step approach you can apply to building expertise and visibility for your firm's chosen industry(ies).

Your employees' career development in their chosen professions has two components. First, they need to establish their foundational technical expertise so they can provide clients with excellent engagement deliverables. They'll be satisfied and rewarded because they have delivered the service for which the firm was paid. But after they build competence and confidence in their basic technical skills, these professionals can work on building knowledge and a network in their focus industry. Their career progress and satisfaction can grow exponentially as they combine technical service delivery skills with confidence and contributions as thought leaders in their chosen industries. Your firm's professionals will gain career satisfaction and will command higher fees because their value to clients goes beyond a service-for-a-fee, transforming them into true business advisors and the client's first choice, at that!

The Firm of the Future is an often-used phrase predicting the attributes of successful firms that can navigate major upheavals and drivers of change in the accounting and consulting industry. Accounting industry thought leaders speak about the accelerating pace of technology that replaces manual processes and procedures with automated processes that increase speed and accuracy while lowering costs for standard accounting firm deliverables. Firms are encouraged to get on board by investing heavily in machine learning, robotic process automation, and artificial intelligence tools to address commoditization of compliance services and the associated pressure to lower fees.

However, investing in technology is only half the battle. Technology is never a magic bullet or a cure-all for all your firm's problems. Technology or IT systems need to be driven by the strategic business goals that drive the forward motion of your firm. If technology is your highest priority to lead change and define success, it's like the tail wagging the dog!

Firms that will survive and thrive must offer clients a compelling reason to be less fee sensitive and value their service provider for the positive attributes their professionals bring to the relationship. When firms focus on investing in building depth and expertise in their clients' industries, they demonstrate their commitment to being a true business advisor and partner their clients will rely on as they face their own business challenges and opportunities. These firms that invest in their professionals and their clients through industry specialization are *the Firms of the Future!*

1.
Greatness Isn't Achieved by Generalists

A firm that cannot distinguish itself using specialization is known simply as a generalist – putting the firm at a definite competitive disadvantage. The firms singled out for achieving accelerated growth most often attribute that growth to specialization. When leadership commits to a specialization strategy, it enables the firm to stay focused and execute that growth strategy.

An industry specialization program can bring blurry and ill-defined growth strategies into sharp focus and clarity! The greater your firm's focus as it strives to achieve its goals, the more efficient, productive and successful your firm can become. Your accounting, tax or consulting professionals should be encouraged to work on strengthening their networks and building or enhancing relationships with clients and prospects. And, if they stay focused on a specific market or industry, your firm will accelerate its growth and success.

The reputation of every professional services firm equals the aggregate of the individual reputations of its professionals. When trying to inspire or coach professionals, I tell them to think of their careers as a journey from generalist to specialist. The more specialized they become, the higher the price they can command for their services and the greater the value they bring to clients.

Specialization Matrix

Specialists have a higher value than generalists in the marketplace.

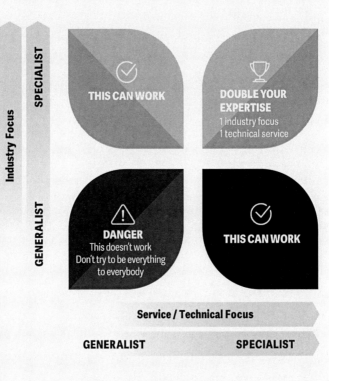

I've coached many professionals through the following career phases

- **Generalist** – As a generalist, often when you begin your career, **your goal** is to provide excellent delivery of basic services for a fee, but those services are highly price sensitive.

- **Technical specialist** – When you've mastered a technical specialty, you are differentiated in the marketplace. Because that skill set is harder to come by, you have fewer competitors, and, therefore, you face less fee-based competition.

- **Industry specialist layered on top of your technical service line specialty** – Maybe you focus on one or two industries, or a large umbrella industry with many niches, like financial services or manufacturing and distribution. Now, you're really distinguished from your competitors. You'll be more highly valued by clients, who are even less likely to focus on the lowest-fee provider.

- **Industry luminary** – Just a few practitioners with deep expertise in one industry will become industry luminaries in their spaces – combining both the niche technical expertise with the relevant business acumen that makes them highly valued trusted advisors. Industry luminaries bring clients the highest value and the deepest specialization. Luminaries command higher fees and build deeper, more long-lasting valued relationships with clients and referral sources.

Go Narrow as You Grow

Industry specialization can work for your firm and your firm's professionals. Professionals can become a technical specialist and then layer on an industry specialty or sector specialty too.

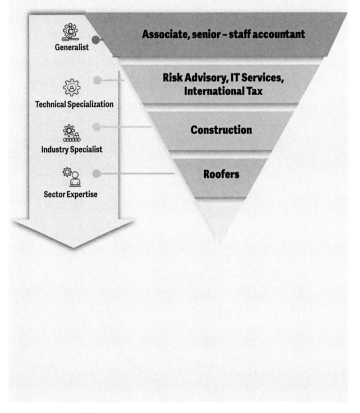

For example, think of your clients as people with specific medical ailments. My mother has cataracts. My father broke his hip. My brother has a severe rash. None of these medical problems can be helped by a generalist. My mother, father, and brother each need to see a different specialist. They each want and need to see the right specialist who has the deep expertise that's relevant to their specific medical issues.

It's the same with your clients, each with challenges and opportunities unique to their specific business, industry and market. One client is a restaurant, another client a construction company, and a third client is an auto parts manufacturer. Each client lives and breathes its own business in the context of its specific industry, facing direct competitors in their own markets. There is no way a generalist can bring the same value to the client as a specialist in that client's industry. Each of these clients will gravitate toward a professional services firm where their own industry is well understood and already known among competitors in their industry.

A firm that cannot distinguish itself using specialization is known simply as a generalist – putting the firm at a definite competitive disadvantage. The firms singled out for achieving accelerated growth most often attribute that growth to specialization. When leadership commits to a specialization strategy, it enables the firm to stay focused and execute that growth strategy.

Reality Check

Strategies for supporting industry groups with limited resources

Big Four firms enjoy the luxury of having sophisticated internal resources dedicated to each industry practice team. Smaller firms with smaller budgets can learn from the Big Four, since even at the megafirms, all resources have their limits. Firms with smaller budgets can still learn from the examples set by larger firms, although they need to adjust implementation based on their own available resources. At the Big Four firm where I worked, the industry program evolved and improved with each new iteration. When I was a senior knowledge manager for the national real estate leadership team, a host of changes occurred as the industry program moved to version 2.0. As the firm's smallest industry, real estate wasn't offered a fully built-out, dedicated support team. Other larger industry groups were supported by the following:

- a dedicated professional researcher/writer to research and author thought leadership articles,
- a dedicated market intelligence researcher,
- a full-time national marketing manager to develop and lead execution of the marketing strategy,
- executive assistant to pull financial reports for the

practice and produce PowerPoint presentations and internal communications for the national industry leader, and

- a full-time senior manager who maintained that industry's internal knowledge site on the firm's intranet platform.

In addition, larger industry teams developed robust courses and fully built-out training supported by a professional from the firm's learning and organizational development department.

My real estate practice support team, on the other hand, had just three dedicated resources – a marketing manager, a senior knowledge manager (me), and an executive assistant/financial manager. There was also a partially dedicated market intelligence professional who helped with thought leadership and competitive analysis.

So, how did the real estate practice survive and thrive with fewer resources? Everyone pitched in and wore multiple hats. As knowledge manager, I also helped produce thought leadership articles, internal communications/newsletters and competitive analysis; facilitated strategy workshops for the national real estate leadership team; and identified internal and external real estate training courses and resources who could fill in the gaps. The official job, "real estate knowledge manager," was my primary responsibility, but our industry leader made it clear that pitching in to help with all the functions where resources were scarce would be key to my success in this role.

Tactics that helped us achieve extraordinary output with very limited resources included:

1. *Leveraging thought leadership articles produced by other industries and tailoring them to the real estate industry.* Eighty percent of the work was typically already done, and just twenty percent needed customization for the real estate industry.

2. *Squeezing the juice out of external resources.* The real estate national leader already had membership in the most important real estate professional associations. These associations all had extensive resources on their websites, enabling me to identify external learning opportunities and make them available to the practice.

3. *Using contests, rewards, and recognition to motivate audit, tax and consulting practitioners to become thought leaders and prolific authors, speakers and leaders of the firm's local office real estate practices.* This was a win-win for the firm and individual professionals who built their expertise and reputations in the marketplace. Accountants don't have to be great writers, but once they provide their expertise, marketing can add the necessary review and editing input.

4. *Creating internal learning course content to develop lower-level professionals into future industry thought leaders by leveraging industry professionals' time.* We also provided part-time support to professionals by getting buy-in and help from the firm's internal learning

organization. This was a partnership between the firm's industry expert, who shared industry technical or business knowledge, and the firm's training team, which understood the principles of curriculum and course development.

> **Summing It Up**
>
> The more you specialize, the greater your value in the marketplace, and the less price sensitive your clients will be. This is true for each professional and for the firm as a whole. There are many different ways to specialize and a career path can be a journey towards deeper and narrower industry and/or technical expertise or layering on an industry specialty and a technical specialty.
>
> Each kind of specialization is a differentiator and great asset for your firm, but it's important to distinguish between service specialties and industry specialties. If all your firm's professionals are aware of the depth and breadth of your firm's service offerings and industry specialties, cross-selling and serving the full needs of your clients will be easier to accomplish. All these specialties can convert to strong revenue growth as your professionals' and your firm's reputation for expertise grows in the marketplace.
>
> It's necessary to invest in marketing tactics aimed at industry and service specialty reputational branding. But there are excellent tactics to successfully market your specialties with a limited financial investment and minimal marketing resources. And even limited investments and resources need to be managed wisely, with an eye towards return on investment (ROI).

2.

Your Industry Program's Value Proposition

Industry specialization allows your firm to command a higher price for its services and bring greater value to your clients.

When I've asked clients whether they perceive a real difference between their own accounting firm and their direct competitors, the most common answer was "no." The expectation is that most firms are on an even playing field when it comes to doing the work. Everyone is expected to provide high-quality services, delivered on time, for a competitive fee. In fact, if a firm and its closest competitors are hard to differentiate, clients tend to differentiate based upon price. Naturally, being known as the lowest-cost provider is not the reputation you want for long-term sustainable growth.

Industry specialization is a differentiation strategy focused on the professionals who comprise your firm. It's about each of their careers and their personal growth. The industry strategy that benefits the firm's professionals also benefits the firm. The four key differentiators explored below refer to the firm, and they are also the key differentiators for each professional in the firm. The firm's reputation and brand promise are really based on the collective reputations earned by the firm's professionals.

What value proposition are you offering your clients? What separates your firm from the competition? What do you want to be known for? Clients say the four differentiators I've highlighted in the list below add "value." Time and again, client feedback discussions reveal how important it is for a firm to demonstrate a dedication to the client's industry to win their business and build a deep and long-lasting relationship with that client.

Four Ways to Differentiate Your Firm

1. **Bring a deep understanding and perspective of the client's business in the context of their industry.** Companies lean toward service providers that don't need a primer to gain a basic understanding of their business model and how it fits into the framework of its suppliers, customers and competitors.

2. **Be proactive. Anticipate the client's needs**, sometimes even before the client knows they have a need. Again, this requires a deep understanding of the client's industry, the economic trends, outlook for the future, and the prevailing business environment that impacts the client's challenges and opportunities.

3. **Offer your client industry insights to demonstrate your firm's client-centric focus.** Do this whether the content is developed by thought leaders within your firm or you're sharing externally published industry information. Both kinds of content are important in demonstrating your commitment to your

The Four Differentiators

Industry expertise is the primary driver behind all four differentiators needed for clients to recognize the value-add beyond the services your firm provides.

client. Sharing industry insights is the primary way your firm can establish itself and its professionals as thought leaders and experts in your client's industry.

4. **Bring the right team.** Engagements should be led and staffed by professionals who not only have the technical expertise to accomplish the work and deliver services, but who also possess the relevant industry experience, knowledge and expertise to act as valued and trusted advisors.

Professional services marketing firm Hinge completed a study in 2017 to uncover the differences between high-growth professional services firms and average-growth firms. Here are a few key findings:

The Hinge study revealed the fastest-growing firms were 89 percent more likely to build and proactively demonstrate their areas of industry expertise.

Time and again, client feedback discussions reveal how important it is for a firm to demonstrate a dedication to the client's industry to win their business and build a deep and long-lasting relationship with that client.

The difference between high-growth and average-growth firms lies in their marketing. For instance, most firms that serve a wide range of clients in businesses where the firm has no particular industry expertise are growing at a slower rate than specialists. In fact, *specialists grew twice as fast*. And how a firm differentiates itself has a measurable impact on its growth rate. In short, the marketing decisions you make can dramatically affect your firm's growth and profitability. What's a buyer's single most important criterion when selecting a professional services firm? According to the Hinge research study, expertise is the clear winner. In fact, expertise tips the scale in favor of a firm in three out of four cases. In addition, expertise is cited as the factor most likely to generate referrals – it's even more powerful than client referrals!

The fastest-growing firms go to great lengths to improve and demonstrate their expertise, according to the Hinge study. They adopt specific strategies that raise the profile of the firm's expertise at the firm, practice, and individual levels. These strategies include writing and speaking on topics of intense interest to their clients. And they include using promotional techniques that expose the firm's expertise to audiences beyond their immediate locale, from search engine optimization to social media to partner marketing.

Source: 2017 Hinge High Growth Study

Beat the Competition!

Specialization is a differentiator, but it's becoming table stakes today. This means specialization is not optional, it's expected in today's competitive marketplace. Clients expect more from accounting, tax and consulting firms than excellent service delivery. Clients expect their service providers to truly understand their industry. Commoditization of services and the resultant fee pressure compels every firm to identify unique differentiators that clients perceive as value-adds, above and beyond the actual services delivered. The importance of providing a differentiated client experience is evolving as a best-in-class strategy for firms striving to achieve sustainable growth.

Competition is driving the strongest firms toward greater and deeper industry specialization. Every firm, however, designs and executes its industry strategy in a way that is unique and distinct from its competitors, depending on the individual strengths of its own culture and mix of professionals. While competitive intelligence can provide useful information, your firm's industry strategy will be a unique presentation to the marketplace. It will be driven by the particular industry strengths your professionals contribute to building your firm's reputation for depth of expertise in your chosen industries.

Reality Check

The real estate practice, as a gold standard industry at RSM

Ten years ago, as I sat in a conference room with national industry leaders at RSM, I heard the magic words that made a pivotal impact on my thinking about the power of industry specialization. This experience opened my eyes to the essence and very core of how your firm's industry strategy can turn your practice from good to great.

RSM's national real estate industry leader, Rick Edelheit, was speaking about one of his most important clients, the strengths and complexity of its business model, its challenges and successful growth trajectory.

I interrupted with a simple question. "Rick, is that client an audit or tax client or perhaps we provide advisory services?" Rick's answer was also simple but powerful. "We think of it, first and foremost, as a real estate client." In other words, his point was that we want to think of our clients holistically, and we want to address each client with a specific suite of services that positions us as a true business partner. We are tied at the hip to this client, fully invested in providing whatever services are needed to help it achieve its business goals. As a practice, all audit, tax and advisory real estate professionals sat together and worked together on real estate clients, on one floor of RSM's Chicago office.

There are two other trademarks of Rick's leadership style that we can all learn from. First, while Rick's personal focus, and that of his local Chicago team, was the very large-scale real estate funds, which is a niche within real estate, acting as a national leader, Rick embraced, supported and empowered the smaller but growing real estate teams emerging across RSM's other regions and markets.

He stepped up his own game as leader of a broader, more diverse practice rather than touting his own highly lucrative book of business. Rick was a strong believer in consciously building camaraderie and deep trust among his team members that crossed the common work boundaries based on service lines and geographic markets. Establishing a regular cadence of in-person meetings, while periodically taking regional real estate team leaders away from the demands of billable time was essential to building a strong team.

I saw multiple marquee client wins that Rick touted as achievable only because of this united and collaborative approach. Rick confidently contends that he would not have won the business on his own; the team approach was essential to winning. Rick would speak of this example to showcase what his close-knit but diverse team could achieve. This was more important to Rick, as an industry leader, than showcasing his own abilities as a rainmaker,

Second, but also important to RSM's real estate practice, was including a very strong sales asset in the real estate team. A business developer, who himself was deeply knowledgeable and networked in the real estate community, was embedded in Rick's team. This wonderful asset worked hand in hand with the real estate team's dedicated marketing leader (who also built her career inside the real estate industry) to create and execute a powerful marketing and sales strategy that worked to achieve outstanding revenue growth.

Lessons learned:

1. Focusing on the client, with confidence that you and your team truly understand the business drivers in its industry, will allow you to change your mindset from thinking of the client as an audit or tax client to thinking of it as a real estate client, or a construction client, or a food or beverage client. When the client's business and its place in its industry are of prime importance, the right mix of service engagements will follow.

2. While most firms select industry leaders who are successful rainmakers, the best industry leaders are rainmakers who also are great leaders of people and teams.

They know that being a successful leader takes them beyond the world of their own clients or book of business and requires them to foster and enable collaboration, based on trust between partners.

3. Many accounting firms rely on business developers ("BDs") to open doors and help partners develop warm leads. Everywhere I've worked, I've seen that some BDs are highly successful, and some are abysmal failures, and they come and go. But often firms see BDs as versatile, covering geographic markets or territories, like sales reps in many industries. These BDs may be charming, aggressive and know how to close a deal. But they often have no deep expertise in any one industry or target market. Those skilled BDs who are known to a specific industry community, who can talk the talk and know the latest issues impacting the target's industry are, overall, far more successful.

Summing It Up

When listening to accounting, tax, and advisory firm clients, we hear over and over that firms that are direct competitors are very hard to differentiate based on the quality of the deliverables. Most are delivering work products that come up to expected industry standards. When we hear clients talk about true differentiators between firms, we listen closely. Time and again, clients tell us that it is important to them that the service providers they choose truly understand their businesses in the context of their competition in their specific industry. They want an engagement team staffed by professionals with the right technical and industry expertise. Clients want a working relationship with a partner who proactively delivers industry insights and knowledge about their industry and their competition. These are the kinds of differentiators that are proven value-adds, above and beyond the service your firm provides.

3.
Walk a Mile in Your Clients' Shoes

Clients want service providers who know their industry. By serving many organizations within the same industry, your firm can see similarities and differences in their business models and understand how management decisions impact profitability and other nuances that make them more competitive within their industry.

Industry specialization reduces the risk of making errors and maximizes the opportunity to give good advice. It provides a window into the nuances of "business valuation," for example, which are unique to a specific industry, and industry subject matter experts understand it better than someone who is not a specialist.

Firms with industry programs can offer a comprehensive network of professionals to meet clients' needs. You'd choose a cardiologist to treat your heart problems, right? Similarly, a client will choose an accounting/consulting firm that specializes in their industry and lives and breathes it like they do.

My real-life example: *Twenty-four years ago, I had a baby who needed brain surgery, and I was lucky enough to find the number one, nationally known pediatric neurosurgeon right in the children's hospital in my city. After the successful* *surgery, as I was taking my baby to the follow-up visit, I started to wonder how much the surgeon would charge. Thanks to health insurance, I didn't even consider the cost of the doctor's services when selecting the right provider. However, my overriding thought was that I didn't care if the medical bills were a million dollars. Whatever the price, I would have willingly paid it. In fact, the value of these very specialized services was priceless to me!*

This example might seem extreme, *but*, if I started a business and put my heart and soul into building it up, taking risks and depending on it for my family's livelihood, the business would be like "my baby" – and you can bet I'd prefer the service provider who truly understands my business in the context of my industry. The service provider who takes the time to bring the right team and valuable industry insights is the one I'd choose, and I'd be much less price sensitive and unlikely to award the work to the lowest bidder.

When coaching professionals on building strong industry specialization strategies, I've asked them to consider the following questions:

Can you, as an assurance, tax or consulting professional, answer the following questions in the context of your focus industry?

What's happening in the industry?
> What are the recent big deals or transactions in this industry? Are there new regs or tax laws that will impact businesses in this industry – either positively or negatively?

Who are the big industry players?
Who are the industry players prominent in your own markets?

Who are the key bankers, lawyers, and centers of influence who are your referral sources?
Are you actively working on building relationships with some of these referral sources?
Do you have a relationship with the centers of influence?
What industry organizations do you participate in?

Have you written or contributed to any thought leadership articles or performed any speaking engagements?

If you can answer "yes" to some or all of these questions, you are on the path to being, or you already are a preferred and trusted advisor in your chosen industry.

You aren't just someone with technical expertise who's performing a service for which the client is paying a fee. Technical expertise is the baseline required on every engagement. In contrast, industry insights and understanding are the differentiators for your clients.

Industry specialization reduces the risk of making errors and maximizes the opportunity to give good advice. It provides a window into the nuances of "business valuation," for example, which are unique to a specific industry, and industry subject matter experts understand it better than someone who is not a specialist.

 **Reality Check**

Categorizing or mapping clients and billings to specific industries can be tricky.

In the old days, the firms I joined would expect new client information to be entered into a billing or customer relationship management (CRM) system that contained required information fields. One important field was for the client's "industry," which was open to interpretation or the opinion of the partner who acquired that new client. Frequently, the client's industry was entered incorrectly due to lack of true understanding of the client's industry or because of confusion or misinterpretation regarding the client's true business activities. Even worse, when the client's business was in more than one industry, the partner entering the new client information could be biased toward one or another industry designation. Often, no industry designation at all was included in a new client entry, because that information wasn't perceived to be important enough to record.

Accurately recording a client's industry is very important. That's because industry information gives your firm a baseline of the size of each industry practice, enabling the firm to track revenue and other key metrics and an industry practice group's progress toward reaching its growth-rate goals. Your firm services business clients across a broad spectrum of industries. Even though you may not have a formal industry practice group for every industry in the US economy, you need to accurately track each client's industry, and engagement revenues should track to each industry.

The benefits of having this industry information include:

- **Establishing a baseline** (in terms of gross revenue, number of clients, realization and net revenue) for all clients, across all industries, by service line and location. Baselines are the starting points for measuring annual and continuous growth throughout the year.

- **Understanding the relative size of industries** your firm serves. You may find that the firm's largest industry served in terms of gross revenue is private households (or individuals), but this group of clients may have the lowest realization, and, therefore, is relatively less profitable for the firm.

- **Uncovering hidden areas of strength and expertise.** Your firm may have a concentration in an industry or sector within a larger industry that you didn't even realize you had. Once you have this critical information about a hidden strength, your firm may make a strategic decision to invest in building out a formal industry practice group, with a strategic growth plan to leverage the traction you already have in a particular industry.

- **Uncovering gaps or problems** – your data can reveal industries where cross-selling is already strong, or industries that are ripe for cross-selling specialty services but where the firm isn't currently focusing its efforts on doing so.

A **best practice** is to map your firm's clients into industry buckets by using the NAICS codes, which look at the client's business through the eyes of the outside business marketplace and not through the subjective eyes of partners entering a new client into your CRM or billing system.

NAICS (pronounced "nakes") codes are classifications within the North American Industry Classification System developed for use by federal statistical agencies for the collection, analysis and publication of statistical data related to the US economy. Adopted in 1997 in cooperation with the statistical agencies of Canada and Mexico, it replaced the standard industrial classification (SIC) system, with the goal of establishing a North American standard. The NAICS was the first economic classification system based on a single economic concept. The most recent revisions and updates to the NAICS code system were in 2017, resulting in 1,057 six-digit NAICS codes.

The NAICS system allows for more flexibility than the former classification system's four-digit structure. It uses a hierarchical six-digit coding system, classifying all economic activity into 20 different industry sectors. Five of these sectors are primarily those that produce goods, while the remaining 15 sectors provide some type of service. Every company receives a primary NAICS code, indicating its main line of business. This primary code is determined by the code definition that generates the largest revenue for a company at a specified location in the past year.

There are numerous free resources on the internet where you can capture your client's NAICS codes. For a fee, you can even automate the flow of your clients' NAICS codes into your system of record. Your firm has the flexibility to make minor modifications regarding which NAICS codes map to the industry practice groups, depending on the strategic focus of each of these groups.

Using the NAICS code systems provides your firm with an objective source of your clients' industry information. You'll achieve greater accuracy with less debate and fewer inconsistencies.

Summing It Up

In this modern world, where so many services are automated and commoditized, it has become the age of specialization in so many domains. The question is not whether to specialize in industries, but what is the best way to get started and set up for success in your mission to develop and deliver industry specialization to your clients and targets. One essential tool in your firm's toolbox is using the NAICS code system to identify the industries of your clients and targets. The accurate mapping of your clients to all industries, but in particular, the industries your firm chooses for its focus, is an essential part of the launching pad to get your industry strategy built on a solid foundation.

4.

Specialties and "Client Experience Excellence" Growth Strategies

An industry specialization strategy can provide your CPA/consulting firm with a road map for organic and acquired growth. It is one surefire way to accelerate growth for your firm and your people. Done right, it is a comprehensive strategy in the marketplace where you compete for both clients and talent.

Joined at the hip with industry specialization and a successful industry program are the *talent experience* and the *client experience*. Mirror images of one another, they are also the keys to becoming the successful Firm of the Future. Industry specialization is a primary driver for attracting and retaining both the best talent and preferred clients. Simply put, the two most important assets for any firm are your people and your clients!

You want your firm to be the first choice of the best talent and the best clients. But how do you define "best" for your firm?

Your Firm's Path to Specialization

Specialization is often described as a "niche" or "industry." It's important to be clear that specialty services or narrow technical areas of expertise, while certainly specialties, are *not* industries. These technical specialties and unique service offerings can also be differentiators. Service specialties can be industry agnostic, delivered to clients across a broad range of industries, or just a few, or just one. But service specialties are not industries. As with industries, the services may have a defined target market that crosses industries, but they are *not* industries.

Joined at the hip with industry specialization and a successful industry program are the talent experience and the client experience. Mirror images of one another, they are also the keys to becoming the successful Firm of the Future. Industry specialization is a primary driver for attracting and retaining both the best talent and preferred clients.

For example, an SEC practice focused on serving public companies that require specialized technical expertise is a great differentiator for a firm, but it is not an industry specialty. Companies in many industries that have opted to take the initial public offering (IPO) or special purpose acquisition company (SPAC) route need technical expertise to do so. They also will value a service provider's deep understanding of their specific industry, their competitors, and the impact of the economic environment on their industry and their business. Demonstrating this deep industry expertise, which is layered on top of the technical SEC service line expertise, builds trust and reliance on the service provider's advice.

One reason it's so important to distinguish between service specialties and traditional industry specialties is the great opportunity it opens up for collaboration between these two different practice areas. A firm's industry-focused practices develop important networking relationships, referral sources, and reputations as industry advisors. The industry practices can grow by offering the right mix of specialty services tailored to resonate with that particular industry target market. The collateral benefit is that the specialty service can grow by identifying clients in industries that benefit from that specialty and leveraging the industry practices as a conduit to reaching these industry clients and targets. For example, R&D tax credits are particularly well suited for tech start-ups and food processors. Therefore, the firm's R&D tax credit experts should be encouraged to collaborate with the technology industry and the food and beverage industry teams for introductions to clients or jointly targeting new businesses that are good candidates for R&D tax credits.

Internal messaging to the firm's professionals should make it clear that they can choose a service offering specialty. *Or* they can choose an industry specialty. Examples of service specialties within the tax department are R&D tax credits, cost segregation, international tax, transfer tax, and state and local tax. Within the advisory department, service specialties often include cybersecurity, IT system selections and/or system implementations, and outsourced services such as outsourced IT, accounting, CFO, or HR services. Assurance-related specialties include transaction advisory services (usually including buy-side or sell-side due diligence, and quality of earnings reports), SEC services, and risk advisory services.

Traditional industry specialties include construction, real estate, financial services, food and beverage, healthcare, technology, life sciences, cannabis, nonprofits, government, and education. A broad spectrum of compliance and specialty services can be bundled and targeted to serve companies within these industry groups.

Regardless of which option they choose, the professional is moving from being a generalist to being a specialist. Even better, some professionals will choose to have a dual specialty – in both a service offering and an industry – which will make them even more highly valued in the marketplace, thereby commanding higher fees and strengthening both the firm's and the professional's reputation for deep expertise.

All your firm's professionals need to clearly understand the firm's areas of strength, its chosen industries and service specialties. If everyone understands the depth and breadth of the firm's capabilities, they're better able to draw upon the right expertise for each client. They are also better equipped to assist industry clients in choosing the right array of services to help them achieve their business goals. The result will be enhanced cross-selling and deeper client relationships, yielding a truly differentiated client experience.

While some professionals may choose to become technical specialists, for example, in internal audit, SEC public company filings, or R&D tax credits, most will maintain and periodically update their baseline technical skills with a strong but general set of technical tools in the toolbox. As your firm's professionals begin concentrating on engagements in a specific industry, the nuances of providing the right mix of technical service offerings to clients in that industry becomes more and more evident. This means your professionals can achieve industry specialization with little additional technical skill development.

They create focus by building depth in one target industry. Building knowledge surrounding the nontechnical issues and trends in almost any industry is a highly achievable goal.

As an industry specialist, such a professional becomes better equipped to recognize when their client needs nuanced technical expertise. Then, the professional's job as a client relationship manager is to offer the client that technical expertise, either from colleagues within your firm or, if necessary, outside your firm. This guidebook reveals the easiest and fastest ways to build each professional's reputation as an industry expert who views the client holistically and brings the right mix of services to meet that client's business needs.

Encourage your professionals to follow their passions and joys when choosing an industry or sector focus. Maybe their interest in an industry is based on enjoying or being committed to that industry's products or services. Or maybe they're drawn to the culture, mindset or personalities that make up an industry's marketplace. Regardless, they will be working to become entrenched in an industry community they enjoy and want to support. They will derive satisfaction from becoming a part of its success. As industry-focused professionals, they can then bring their technical skills as an accountant, tax advisor or consultant to help contribute to their clients' successes. A client's satisfaction with your professionals as their trusted advisors will also provide the professionals with career satisfaction. Success breeds more success and deeper involvement with existing and potential clients in that focus industry. This in turn, enhances the individual's reputation and the firm's reputation, based on his or her specialized industry knowledge, and the cycle continues...

Industry Specialization as a Career Path

CPA/professional services firms on sustainable growth trajectories specialize in chosen industries. Industry specialization is also the path to career success for your firm's people.

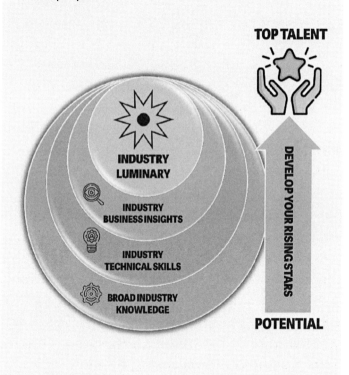

 **Reality Check**

Handling power struggles

Industry leaders are often expected to achieve their goals by "leading through influence rather than authority." Easier said than done. Many CPA/professional service firms' reporting structures and P&L responsibilities are based on geographic and service line hierarchies. The authority and power that comes with the financial burdens of running a business are usually established before management recognizes the importance of industry specialization. Once power is divvied up, it's hard to share it with or reallocate it to another center of influence – namely, the industry practice group leaders.

I joined one large national firm to help build a national industry strategy. The regional managing partners (RMPs) owned the burden of the P&L for their respective regions, which trickled down to the office managing partners (OMPs). RMPs also controlled a regional compensation pool for partner profit sharing each year. The leaders of the service lines, both national and regional leadership, had a well-established hierarchy where professionals in assurance, tax and consulting reported up through the ranks for their annual reviews, raises, bonuses and promotions.

While industry leadership and groups represented the matrixed firm's third leg of the stool, it was the Johnny-come-lately. Unlike RMPs and OMPs, industry national and regional leaders had no responsibility for a true P&L, and no compensation pool to incent professionals to build their respective industries. They also had no professionals who reported directly to them. Industry leaders had no direct influence over annual reviews, raises, bonuses and promotions. Ultimately, industry leaders truly had to lead using influence rather than authority – a major stumbling block to building effective and productive industry teams and professionals.

The firm's senior leaders came to understand that for the industry practice groups to help accelerate the firm's growth, something had to change. They knew at the very core, industries are firmwide or national. Industries cross all offices, all regions and all service lines. Expertise in one of the firm's offices could be leveraged as needed in any of the firm's offices. Regardless of the specific services performed, industry expertise should be brought to the table to win new clients and to better serve existing clients, regardless of the industry professional's service line. In fact, they embraced the concept that "industry should be interwoven into everything we do."

A significant step forward to achieve the goal of building truly national industry practices occurred when the firm's partners agreed to move from a regional partner compensation pool to a national one. This change eliminated the major industry growth hurdles that resulted from competition and hoarding of resources within regions.

Firms new to building industry teams should first consider how to motivate and incent their professionals to advance their careers to the next level with an industry specialty. And while the rewards of industry specialization can be compelling for the firm and its professionals, it doesn't happen overnight. Professionals must stick with their industry focus over time – to develop true expertise and experience so they can deliver insightful and valued advice to their industry clients. Short-term financial and public recognition incentives are essential tactics smart firms have used successfully to overcome power struggles and ensure that professionals are motivated to get on board with changing their mindset about the importance of developing an industry focus for their careers.

Summing It Up

If you are here, it's because you (or your firm) are seeking a roadmap to revenue growth. As a firm managing partner, or an assurance, tax, or advisory professional, you may be searching for an effective strategy to set your firm on a track to achieve extraordinary revenue growth. By blending industry expertise with client experience excellence, your firm can achieve a competitive advantage. In the past, many firms characterized all specialties as "niches" and didn't pay much attention to whether these practice areas were industry specialties or service specialties. It's very important to clarify exactly which areas of your firm's expertise represent service or technical expertise, and which are your firm's traditional industry practices specialties. I hope this chapter has clarified the different kinds of specialties. In turn, it's your responsibility to make sure every professional in your firm knows exactly what your industry specialties are and what your service specialties are. This is the first step to leveraging and achieving ROI on your industry specialization and client experience strategies.

5.

Why You Need Effective Industry Teams and How to Get There

There are immediate and long-term internal and marketplace benefits of establishing industry teams at your firm. Here are some of the important benefits and outcomes the firm will achieve when you establish industry teams across your firm's locations. Your firm will:

- Win more industry clients by demonstrating deep industry experience.

- Build awareness of the importance of industry specialization.

- More easily and systematically share industry insights and knowledge.

- Collaborate internally to produce industry thought leadership.

- Cross-sell the breadth of the firm's services to existing clients.

- Team up with industry subject matter experts to benefit existing clients.

- Enhance career paths for your firm's professionals.

Looking for a proven methodology to get your industry teams off the ground and functioning productively? Start here:

- **First**, establish the right industry focuses for your firm, which may differ from location to location.
- **Next**, appoint the right personnel to lead those industries at the national and regional levels.
- **Then**, you're ready to establish industry teams. Each market's industry leader will coach and support business growth activities focused on a target industry market.
- **Finally**, the firm's market industry leaders, together with that industry's national leader, form a national industry leadership team. The national leadership team is responsible for the strategic direction and financial health of the national industry practice group.

The beauty of industry teams is they are cross-functional. The team is best if it includes professionals from assurance, tax and consulting. The industry team environment is a natural place to break down silos and build collaboration and trust between the different lines of business. Trust is essential when partners are asked to recommend services to their clients that will be delivered by other service lines or lines of business – all outside the sphere of the partner's control. Team members need to trust that service delivery will rise to the same level of service excellence the client has come to expect from the firm. Cross-selling strategies are rarely successful unless there is willing collaboration and great trust between professionals who work in different service lines or lines of business.

The goal and benefit of this cross-functional industry team collaboration is the ability to view the client more holistically. Together, professionals from assurance, tax and consulting can bring the client the right basket of services or solutions to help their business really thrive, not just survive.

In order to collaborate as a team, the team must meet!

Industry groups must hold meetings, and I'll explain why these meetings are imperative to every successful industry program. But first, I'll address the concern every firm's management has: they strive to minimize internal meetings whenever possible.

Most accountants at the firms I advised were predisposed to minimize the number of meetings and the length of meetings. Here's why. Accounting firm professionals at all levels are generally driven to get client work done and bill out for their time. Internal meetings take time and focus away from billable client service. It's not wrong to think of internal meeting time as a distraction that takes away from metrics like utilization and realization. Especially when resources are scarce, meetings take away from the alternative use of every professional's time. Every year, this scarcity of time happens during busy season. Managers, senior managers, directors and partners facing difficult deadlines are under pressure to get client engagement work done.

All internal meetings must add significant value to the firm. Meetings should be designed to be effective and productive and not overly long. Frequency needs to be appropriate to accomplish longer-term goals. Yet, meetings are essential to building a successful industry specialization strategy.

Trust, camaraderie, collaboration, loyalty, and reliability are all built over time as team leaders and team members become familiar with each other's personalities and develop friendships and solid working relationships. Formal meeting protocols are the models that enable meetings to be efficient, but familiarity breeds the team spirit that reinforces the notion that "we are all in this together" and "many hands make light work."

The beauty of industry teams is they are cross-functional. The team is best if it includes professionals from assurance, tax and consulting. The industry team environment is a natural place to break down silos and build collaboration and trust between the different lines of business.

When I've asked industry leaders how the process of designing and executing their industry's strategic plan is progressing, invariably they answer that they have a great plan. The problem is no one on the team is accountable or feels responsible for the execution, and the great bulk of the action plan falls to the leader himself or herself. My next question is, "Who built this strategic plan?" Most often, this terrific industry leader proudly declares how much of his hard work and expertise went into building the strategic plan. And of course, I replied, "The plan you devise yourself is the plan you'll have to implement yourself!"

The team should assemble for its first meeting in person, and its first mission should be to begin developing strong personal and professional relationships and a sense

Industry Teams Require Cross-Functional Collaboration

Industry teams are the essential building blocks of your firm – all you need is a plan.

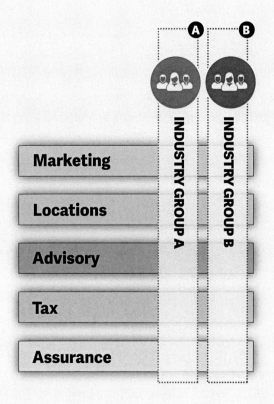

of co-ownership of their common mission and goals. When every team member is an active participant in a strategic planning discussion, the implicit goal is for each team member to feel the imprint of his or her hands on the final plan. Everyone will buy into the plan if they all participated in building it. All team members will act as owners and take responsibility when they are all included; when each person's perspective is heard and respected, and when all participate in prioritizing the activities that the group agrees will help them achieve their joint goals.

Strong professional relationships can't be formed in just one meeting. Trust is built over time and with recognition of successes and offerings of support when needed. To build momentum and reinforce team spirit, you need a natural meeting cadence where growth opportunities for all will be revealed and discussed.

 **Reality Check**

To meet or not to meet?

Meetings that are kept short and to the point, with prepared agendas, discussion topics and planned follow-up actions, are necessary and productive. The types of meetings listed below are important to advance the progress of a firm's industry strategy and, ultimately, accelerate growth based on industry specialization.

- Your firm's national industry leaders should meet as a group of peers to share common challenges or hurdles and offer best practices that will help the group. These meetings should occur at regular intervals, at least twice a year, but also on an as-needed basis.

- Each industry's national industry leadership team should meet in person (highly encouraged) for a full strategic planning workshop. At a minimum, this team should convene in person annually to review successes, compare notes and assessments of the industry practice from the perspective of each geographic market leader, and share insights about current or upcoming industry opportunities. At a minimum, they should also review and refresh their industry strategic plan every two years.

- Each industry's national industry leadership team should also conduct conference calls, Zoom or in-person meetings, if feasible, on a more regular basis. These should be working meetings to report on committee activities, including internal industry training, thought leadership, internal communications and knowledge sharing. These regular meetings should enable each regional or office industry leader to report to the group on business development activities, such as top sales pursuits progressing from leads to qualified opportunities to wins or losses. This is the right forum for discussing existing client cross-selling opportunities and staffing needs for key industry accounts. Operational topics such as standardized client service methodologies, work papers or templates should also be important agenda topics.

- Industry regional or office teams should meet very regularly to execute industry growth strategies at the local level. These local team meetings are where seasoned partners can mentor and coach newer professionals on how to develop a growth mindset, reinforce a positive culture of collaboration, and provide a safe environment for learning and exposure to technical and non-technical topics about their clients' industry.

A strongly encouraged "take one" policy encourages partners, directors or senior managers on industry teams to regularly take a supervisor or manager with them to industry networking events. Starting networking early in their careers encourages professionals to develop a natural comfort level that builds over time. Professionals at all levels and in all service lines can be full contributors to the industry committees where the real work gets done to build the industry training, thought leadership, internal communications and knowledge sharing outlined in the goals established by each industry's national leadership team.

Strong industry team leaders know how important it is to encourage, and in fact require, all meeting attendees to speak up and participate in every meeting. This is true regardless of each team member's seniority or level. Each person should be respected and valued for their contribution, and it is the job of leadership to enable and empower everyone to find a role or task that does make a difference!

The goal of meetings should be to reinforce the behaviors and activities expected to occur between meetings. Participants can all use meeting time to determine informal partnerships to write articles or attend industry networking events together. Pursuit or targeting teams can be formed where several team members work together to win new work. Meeting time can be effective if used to inform the broader group about go-to-market achievements since the last meeting or planning for industry market-facing activities that will occur before the next team meeting.

Summing It Up

Since so much of the purpose and success of your industry strategy depends on strong collaboration and breaking down silos between different work groups at your firm, effective teaming is of critical importance. Teams must meet to build working relationships where all team members are supportive of each other and accountable to each other. The team's accomplishments should be bigger than the sum of its parts; stronger than the aggregate of the efforts of the individual members. Many hands make light work, requiring that every team member be an active contributor.

By definition, teams must meet regularly to establish camaraderie, mutual trust and interdependence. Forward motion and momentum are lost when team meetings lack regularity and continuity. Every meeting should be properly planned to be productive and effective, with deliverables and follow-up plans as part of the routine for each team. Meetings are a place to hold all members accountable to the goals and action plans they set for themselves, and also a place to applaud individual efforts and successes, as well as celebrate the accomplishments of the team.

6.

It's All About Establishing a Growth Mindset

Your firm's long-term viability depends on how successful you are in creating and sustaining a growth culture and mindset. For industry practice groups to succeed at driving growth, they must incorporate and reinforce the firm's growth culture. A firm with an intentional growth culture could articulate the mission as follows:

> *Our firm has a shared set of values and beliefs that guide our professionals in their sales goals, marketing, business development and client relationship expansion activities.*

Professionals should be provided with best practice guidance related to winning new clients and expanding relationships with existing clients. The growth culture captures the importance your firm places on providing clients with an unparalleled client experience founded on a deep understanding of their industries. Your professionals all focus on *deeper penetration* and strengthening relationships with existing clients while working on strategic targets to win new business. Deeper penetration specifically means that when your firm provides multiple and varied services to a client (typically a business client within any industry), you will make more money and become more deeply embedded with the client. That makes it much harder for the client to replace your accounting firm with a lower-cost service provider. It's harder for the client to extricate themselves from the relationship because your firm is so tied into numerous different functions at the client's business. Also, it gives your firm multiple opportunities to showcase the many different services that you can do so well, to meet the client's needs. They will value your firm so much more than if you just do the financial statements or the compliance tax work.

> A growth culture means that everyone in the firm and on the industry teams knows that they all have an obligation to build business for the firm. They make a commitment to make a serious effort to seek out new clients and deepen penetration with existing clients.

Accelerating growth will depend on improving the level of effectiveness of each of your location-based industry teams, which is where much of the energy in your firm's growth activities is focused. Sales skill development and related programs are also very important.

Two ways to ramp up efforts to instill a growth mindset are: 1) observing industry practice teams in action across the firm, and 2) one-on-one interviews with industry team leaders and others involved with organic growth. This will help you identify best practices and uncovered gaps and assist your firm in developing approaches to overcome barriers to success. Industry leadership should also work closely with a few industry teams as initial pilots to learn more and test assumptions. The *elements of an effective growth culture for industry teams* are explained below. Don't be surprised or overwhelmed by the rigorous and robust elements I've recommended here. Most industry teams will have gaps between their current state and best practices, which are then identified as opportunities for improvement in processes, behaviors or learning.

Establishing a Growth Mindset for Industry Team Members

The following program could be implemented in selected locations and industry practices as part of your firm's industry strategy launch plan. It's a pilot program that will help you establish best practices and build out a repeatable model that can be replicated in other locations and across all industry teams. The pilot will help the firm achieve sustainable and meaningful organic growth at a rate above its competitors.

Strategic focus for creating industry teams
Regional managing partners, market leaders, or office managing partners should approve the creation of industry teams. Setting the right tone at the top, with leadership selecting and endorsing the high-priority industries for growth, will set the teams up for success. These industry team selections need to be aligned with firm strategy but not a "one-size fits all" approach. Each region or office market probably has distinct financial and economic conditions that will drive the choices of which industries present the highest growth opportunities.

Teams can be organized according to industry and sector.

Generally speaking, an industry is a broader grouping of clients that naturally share a common industry umbrella, such as financial services. Many firms will find there is a critical mass of clients at a deeper sector level, such as banking, under the financial services umbrella. From the client's perspective, the sector level is always more relevant, because business clients see their own world as composed of companies that are their direct competitors, or their own customer target market. But at your firm, it may not be possible to go so narrow with deep expertise in every sector. Achieving the balance of expertise at the industry level, and even deeper expertise at the sector level, will look different for every firm. Balance the number of teams in each region or office based on their relative strengths/resources and market opportunity. In other words, don't bite off more than you can chew!

Effective industry team leaders
Regional managing partners or office managing partners should select regional industry team leaders who have demonstrated growth ability. They should be subject matter experts in their industry or sector and be active in geographic referral communities (such as lawyers or bankers relevant to their industry). They should have strong leadership skills, including: high energy, "walks the halls," a passion for growth, and being a leader by example. For more details about the required attributes of outstanding industry team leaders, see the REALITY CHECK at the end of this chapter.

Engaged industry team members
With the approval of the regional or office managing partner,

the industry team leader selects or recruits team members. Industry teams should include a manageable number of people (optimally, six to 12 professionals), all personally committed to growth. All major lines of business (i.e., assurance, tax and consulting) should be represented along with marketing, a business developer (if available and appropriate), and administrative resources.

Regular and productive working meetings should be scheduled for each industry team. Smaller subcommittees that drive the workstreams or tactical plans for the group can be established for larger teams, which is where the real work gets done. Then meetings are useful opportunities to exchange ideas, report back on progress, and commit to further work, either individually or in smaller subcommittees.

The extended industry team includes every professional at every level and within every service line who is committed to building their industry expertise and reputation and contributing to growth of the industry practice. Meetings of this broader group should occur from time to time, with broader groups meeting for training/education and networking.

Organize team meetings with standard practices
The industry team leader should run formal meetings, using a written agenda with a core format. Every meeting should have a set of standard topics, common to all meetings. Of course, special topics come up and should be included and addressed by the team. One core topic of focus is what is in process with the group's high-priority targets and current opportunities. This requires high-priority targets to be established during one of the early meetings. Divvying up these

high-priority targets among the partners in the group, with each partner establishing "pursuit teams" for these targets, is also among the first jobs the industry team must complete.

Other standard topics for industry team meetings should include group and individual participation in industry conferences, trade association meetings or training events, and the potential for the firm's industry group to sponsor their own industry event for clients and targets to attend. These market-facing activities could be a combination of in-person and virtual or hybrid events.

Meeting participants should have the opportunity to speak to their progress or contributions to winning new targets and market activities, and/or authorship of thought leadership articles or presentations. Everyone should leave meetings with an action item, and minutes of the meeting should be distributed. Meetings should last no longer than one hour and be held monthly or bi-weekly, and year-round.

Emphasis on prioritizing of targets for each industry team
The industry team leader steers the process to select the highest-priority target accounts – those with potential to become top clients. There should be a manageable number of "Priority 1" targets per team (10 to 20). This target list should include prospects and existing clients with potential for cross-selling. Each industry team is responsible for developing Priority 1 targets to increase revenues with new clients and expand work with existing clients. Smaller "target teams" with one to two partners leading the charge and other team members who are in roles from managers through directors, can make up the team. Priority 2 and 3 targets should also

be identified. The Priority 3 targets should be monitored by marketing personnel, where available.

Industry team integration with marketing and firmwide strategies and programs
Marketing should facilitate the targeting process and develop programs to help drive the progress of Priority 1 to 3 targets and existing clients. When available, business developers should also help with targeting and facilitating concrete plans to develop each Priority 1 target and drive the pursuit of some Priority 2 accounts. Industry teams should leverage other firmwide strategies, such as experts in other aligned industries, lines of business growth tactics, client experience programs (described in detail in Chapters 9 and 10), and innovative pricing strategies to create momentum and drive growth. Industry team leaders and other partners should leverage sales skills development programs by acting as mentors to less experienced team members.

Industry teams are accountable for results, and "tone at the top" is the critical element
Regional or office managing partners are in the best position to create a culture of accountability. Since these leaders control hiring, firing, performance feedback, bonuses and salary increases, all partners and those who report to partners are usually highly tuned in to the expectations of these leaders. The industry leaders in each region or office should directly report their results to their respective leaders. The industry results should be reported regularly, either quarterly or at a minimum of three times per year.

Leadership should establish clearly defined, measured and monitored success metrics for each team. The metrics need to include lookbacks, which are the measures of financial success every firm relies on to determine whether growth occurred in the prior period (either monthly, quarterly or annually). Most firms use key performance indicators that include gross revenue, realization, and net revenue. Using the firm's data, viewed through an industry practice lens, allows each industry practice group to look back to determine period-over-period growth, and whether growth rate goals were met.

Other metrics should measure forward-looking or "leading" indicators, which are activity and behavior based. The industry teams should track and measure the quality and quantity of thought leadership it produces, and the frequency of public relations opportunities – being quoted in news and trade publications, or interviewed on business and news programs. Other market-facing activities, such as providing industry insights through virtual webcasts or in-person speaking slots at industry conferences or firm-sponsored tent-pole events, are all high priorities and measures of accomplishments for industry teams.

Who should be included in accountability? Everyone involved in the industry groups, from team members through the team leader and local or regional leadership.

Internal communications that endorse a growth strategy through building industry specialization and industry teams with consistency and appropriate frequency will reinforce this shift to a growth mindset.

 **Reality Check**

Industry leaders are groomed – not born.

All professional services firms – the Big Four, the top 100 accounting firms, or small, narrowly focused boutique firms – have one thing in common: The leadership skills of their industry practice leaders will make or break the success of their industry teams.

I've tried, with little to no success, to coach industry leaders who were anointed to lead an industry solely due to the leader's outstanding ability as a rainmaker. Sometimes the perception is that he/she needs the "leader" title on the business card to credentialize capabilities to pursue new clients. Or maybe the industry leader role was promised to the partner as a condition of joining the firm. If the person has no real interest in or the skills for enabling and empowering others to achieve their goals to become known industry experts, it will not work. Instead, it can lead to a toxic culture, with attrition and apathy in the industry practice. The best-case scenario is the creation of work-arounds where others step up to lead, trying to compensate for the actual industry leader's weaknesses.

The reverse is also true. In every firm in which I've worked, the most effective and productive industry teams always have outstanding industry leaders at the helm. These leaders talk the talk and walk the walk. They are distinguished role models of business development, known as go-to thought leaders in the industry, and highly networked in their industry communities. But just as important, they are highly effective at grooming and coaching their team members to follow in their footsteps. They use both the carrot and the stick – knowing how to hold people accountable to their commitments and recognizing their accomplishments. These outstanding leaders are incredibly open to coaching and learning more about best practices regarding leading teams and becoming the best industry leaders to motivate the team and all its members toward their joint and individual goals.

Accounting, tax, and consulting professionals aren't all cut from the same cloth. Some are great at client relationships. Retaining and deepening client relationships is their greatest strength. A very few are outstanding rainmakers. They're able to generate extraordinary revenue and numerous new clients. Then, there are the professionals well-known for their meticulous attention to detail and technical expertise to ensure excellence in engagement deliverables. Some partners or company leaders are terrific at mentoring, coaching and developing their people, and they derive great satisfaction from helping the next generation build their careers.

These are the finders, the minders and the grinders. In many firms, partly out of necessity, partners or company leaders are expected to fill all roles at once. The smarter firms allow those who gravitate to business development to spend most of their time on what they do well. Those who are great process-oriented team leaders are allowed to concentrate on leading teams and engagements. And the highly technical are best utilized where their strongest skills lie, in ensuring that firm quality control is maintained.

Attributes of Outstanding Industry Leaders

What qualities are most valuable in a successful industry practice group leader, whether a national or regional/local office leader? It's a combination of multiple skills.

- **Outstanding rainmaking skills** – Top industry leaders lead by example and consistently win new clients in their chosen industry. Industry specialization is, at its core, a go-to-market strategy for firm growth. The best industry leaders are role models who showcase how winning new clients can and should be done. If the firm's mantra is "no one can coast, and all partners/execs must contribute to growth," then the industry leader has to be able to walk the walk, as well as talk the talk. Monopolizing all the recognition (and financial rewards) for new client wins, rather than enabling and empowering team members to hone their own business development skills, however, is counterproductive to the goals of an effective team.

- **Being recognized as a thought leader** – Any firm with industry leaders who have reputations as eminent or distinguished thought leaders espousing powerful industry insights is extremely fortunate to have this strong differentiator. Industry leaders who are prolific authors of thought leadership articles, and frequent speakers or presenters, are compelling role models for the professionals they lead. This attribute needs to be leveraged through coaching team members to also become thought leaders. Acting as the overall industry thought leader/role model while also encouraging every team member

Industry + Client Growth = Increased Revenue

Everyone in the firm must develop a growth mindset that recognizes the critical importance of industry to your firm and its clients. Business development skills nurtured as an integral part of industry practice group training and deeply embedded in firm culture yield accelerated growth for your firm.

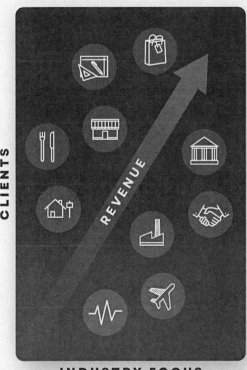

to make contributions to thought leadership is a winning combination.

- **Great networkers in their chosen industry** – Outstanding industry leaders have spent years out in their respective industries' watering holes, at conferences and trade association meetings, building relationships up, down and across the community surrounding their industry's ecosystem. But industry leaders who also bring along staff, managers and senior managers to every industry event are grooming rising industry stars beginning in the early stages of their careers. Enabling young professionals to experience "working the room" and helping them learn how to hobnob with their industry peers is an essential part of industry leadership.

- **Experienced at running an effective and productive organization** – Strong industry leaders know how to manage people, processes and systems to optimize the use of non-billable time. While regular internal meetings are essential, they should be kept short and businesslike so as not to deter from billable activities. All participants must be expected to contribute during meetings. A meeting where the industry leader does all the talking, allowing others to hide, is ineffective. The industry leaders should encourage every participant to be an active member of the team.

Summing It Up

Industry specialization, supported through the vehicle of industry teams with industry leaders, can turn a differentiator into extraordinary revenue growth for the firm. But firms that convert industry focus into more new clients and expanded work for existing clients achieve this goal by infusing a growth culture in the industry teams. A growth culture means that everyone in the firm and on the industry teams knows that they all have an obligation to build business for the firm. They make a commitment to make a serious effort to seek out new clients and deepen penetration with existing clients.

Strong industry leadership skills can make or break the success of every industry team at your firm. And the strongest industry leaders enable and empower their team to integrate a growth mindset and commitment as they build their reputations for deep industry expertise in the marketplace.

7.

Coaching Your People through the Industry Specialization Process

Talent development coaching focused on creating Industry Luminaries is critical to every firm's industry strategy. Becoming an **Industry Luminary**, known for specialization in specific industries, is a multifaceted process. Industry specialization should be purposefully woven into all aspects of your firm: operations, firm culture, metrics and benchmarks, individual performance reviews and incentives for professionals at all levels, as well as marketing and sales strategies.

A successful industry strategy resides on both sides of the same coin. The first is developing people with deep industry expertise and empowering them with the tools to make that happen, while also demonstrating that industry specialization offers a career growth opportunity for many. This is the side of the coin designed to create industry expertise. Just as important is converting that industry expertise into becoming known Industry Luminaries in the marketplace. First, we need experts – then we need to empower them to become known Industry Luminaries.

Once their expertise is in place, we also need the other side of the coin – the market-facing side. On that side, each industry practice team and its members have a few key responsibilities:

- **Industry Luminaries should be able to describe their target market.**
  Which sectors within the umbrella industry is each team pursuing, what part of the broad "middle market" is the sweet spot for each industry team? The more specifically your group can define its target market, the greater the group's clarity, focus and efficiency. Narrowing the focus of your industry's growth strategy also provides you and your team with a better understanding of what you are *not* going to do, which companies in the target industry require you to reach too low or too high and will just distract you from your primary goal. Keeping a clear focus is the key to achieving your team's goals.

- **Industry Luminaries must understand the competitive landscape.**
  For each industry, know who the national and local competition is, and in what niches or target niche markets the competition is playing. Also, scour the competition's websites, press releases and presence in the industry marketplace to gain insight into which industry hot topics and trends they deem it important to address. This vital information lets you know which topics you can't afford to ignore. It also lets you identify the white space, or which topics you can jump on first and "own." These are the industry insights you and your firm can become known for within each industry community.

- **Industry Luminaries need to determine where to engage with the players in their industry and be present in those places.**

  Locate the community or networking venues of each industry. Each industry practice group must make it the business of the team to be active participants in the relevant industry trade association conferences, breakfast clubs, training events, and proverbial industry "hangouts." The industry leader should reinforce the importance of this industry-focused self-marketing with your firm's young talent. One way is to actively participate in and encourage "take one" programs to initiate younger team members in the art of networking in their chosen industry.

- **Industry Luminaries need to showcase their personal industry eminence and your firm's reputation as a thought leader.**

  Becoming credentialed in your industry happens in a variety of ways. Your industry leaders and their teams should leverage their own industry knowledge and expertise by producing content for your firm's website, firm-hosted webcasts or industry events. These investments in time reap rewards and proven ROI because you will build a reputation as the go-to firm for specific industry communities.

Firms need to place industry focus on the front burner for young new partners, mid-career partners who may just now be stepping up to the challenge of building an industry focus,

Essential Components of an Industry Learning Strategy

Becoming a firm/professional with known industry specialties is a multi-faceted process. Establish a strong foundation and build from there.

- Formal courses
- Industry Lunch & Learns
- Industry intranet sites for knowledge sharing

- Work on clients in your industry
- Shadow on sales calls
- Present internally & externally

- Associations
- Industry conferences
- Referral sources
- Industry team collaboration

and particularly for managers, senior managers, and directors. Firms can achieve this culture change by offering their people a career path to partner through industry teams, coaching, and tools to motivate and empower them to follow a career growth path through industry specialization.

Your firm's success with developing Industry Luminaries will depend on how well the firm integrates industry throughout its matrixed organization. The industry strategy can only be executed with the support and empowerment of the firm's leadership and multifaceted support organization, including IT, human resources, learning and organizational development, and marketing.

> Becoming an **Industry Luminary**, known for specialization in specific industries, is a multifaceted process. Industry specialization should be purposefully woven into all aspects of your firm: operations, firm culture, metrics and benchmarks, individual performance reviews and incentives for professionals at all levels, as well as marketing and sales strategies.

Changing the firm's mindset to prioritize industry will accelerate when:

- Industry groups have access to the essential tools and systems that empower productivity, efficiency, collaboration, accountability, and transparency.

- Each national industry group's go-to-market strategy includes enhanced thought leadership programs, brand awareness and digital campaigns, requiring

- a close partnership between industry and the firm's marketing leadership and experienced marketing professionals.

- Industry specialization is closely tied to cultivating the firm's talent. The firm needs to provide employees with the inspiration and tools to build their careers by developing industry expertise. Partnering and leveraging the deep expertise of HR leadership and the firm's learning and organizational development leader is essential to achieving the firm's industry strategy.

Industry learning strategies for your professionals

Offering your firm's professionals a path to developing an industry specialty demonstrates your commitment to the successful growth and development of your firm's most precious asset – your talent! This commitment is also a great tool for your recruiters, who are searching and competing for talented professionals to join your firm at every level and for every service line.

There are many ways your professionals can learn about their industry and stay up-to-date regarding the important industry issues and trends impacting your client. While the firm should offer formal industry training (and of course, technical service line training), learning isn't restricted to the classroom. There are many ways to learn. In addition to formal learning, learning also includes on-the-job experience and information, tips and suggestions you receive from the connections you make, all expanding your industry knowledge.

Learning through "connections" – networking with internal colleagues and connections outside the firm, in places where you find the businesspeople in a focus industry, provides professionals with their best learning opportunities.

The journey from generalist to specialist

Your firm already understands the importance of differentiating itself from the competition by moving from being a firm of generalists to being a firm with a chosen and limited focus on specific industries and technical specialties. (See Chapters 1 and 2.)

However, from a learning and development viewpoint, your firm must provide young professionals with a clear vision of their career pathway. They need to see the light at the end of the tunnel and make sense of the value they bring to the firm, where they currently stand in their own career development process and what the future could hold.

Some of your professionals have already moved significantly down the path to industry specialization, but many are just beginning their journey.

A knowledge management program and the right technology are the keys to effectively sharing your firm's assets and capabilities.

My first role in the internal support world at a Big Four firm was as senior knowledge manager for the national real estate practice group. I was responsible for the intranet portal and its subpages – just one piece of the firm's vast web of internal knowledge-sharing capabilities. The intranet, with its knowledge-sharing capabilities, is an essential tool for every industry practice group. The knowledge management (KM) department at a Big Four firm typically has upwards of 300 people and uses a multidiscipline team approach, including: IT technical support for the knowledge-sharing software platform, platform designers, and dedicated knowledge manager professionals for the intranet subpages that enable each department or function to share and champion distribution of content. The day-to-day work of each internal- and external-facing function and every practice group or team is more efficient, productive and accurate when supported by a well-managed intranet portal.

Although I was a knowledge manager for only one year, I learned best practices shared between and on behalf of the entire KM organization. It was eye-opening. I learned how critically important technology is in implementing a strong KM strategy for any firm bigger than five to 10 professionals, or one with more than one office location or more than two service offerings. The greater the firm's size and complexity, the more important KM becomes to supporting the growth and success of the firm.

To successfully implement your firm's industry strategy, a KM function is vital. KM is really the 21st-century version of library science, which enables the systematic collection of all forms of content and an organized collection and distribution platform, so content is appropriately shared across the organization. The entire enterprise, across all internal- and external-facing functions, needs to be connected so everyone can access the necessary intellectual content and each other. The firm's intranet is the primary IT tool, accessible only to employees or trusted insiders. Sensitive or proprietary content can be curated, cleansed and shared with the members of your internal audience.

A conscientious governance plan is also needed as a guidebook, providing the rules of the road regarding what and how materials get posted and shared. For example, certain kinds of content, such as recent proposals or lists of clients that approve the use of their names in proposals may change and are difficult to monitor for current accuracy. A governance committee may determine that a simple notice reminding the firm's professionals not to reuse proposals or client references without new approval of specific information isn't good enough. The governance or KM guidelines may choose to limit risk by not sharing this content internally, even if it is cleansed of client-sensitive information. In this case, the governance committee will recommend alternative content that helps proposal writers without risking stale or inaccurate information leaving the firm.

KM also enables and empowers communities of practice. The development of communities of practice is important in firms where departmental silos exist that thwart growth strategies like industry specialization. Each industry practice group is a community of practice that crosses the firm's matrix. This typical firm matrix is primarily composed of the work groups and reporting structure formed by the different lines of business and the different offices or geographic regions that make up the firm. These natural boundaries create silos and inhibit collaboration. The industry communities of practice cross geographies (the firm's office locations), cross service line groups, and cross the world of internal- and external-facing departments. As members of these industry teams work to build trust, collaboration and camaraderie, their intranet portals can help. Offering instant internal communications capabilities, the industry intranet portal helps build pride in the group's accomplishments, and informally educates the team about the latest trends and the economic environment that affects industry clients and prospects, making the whole team smarter and more successful.

Knowledge management can be implemented and valuable at smaller firms, too!
Smaller firms can initiate and build the KM function as the firm grows and the need for knowledge sharing expands. All you need to begin is one knowledge manager who has the necessary IT support to launch and maintain the intranet software. It's also possible to outsource this function as an expense rather than add resources to the firm's payroll. But even with outsourcing, there should be someone in a leadership role who understands and champions the importance of knowledge management as a critical driver of the firm's success.

Of course, every firm rightly believes its most important assets are its people. Focusing on building and developing deep expertise and industry experts within the firm is, after all, the aim of this book! For the greater good of the firm, however, industry thought leaders need to spread their wisdom to others and make it readily available to their colleagues at the firm and to the firm's clients and prospects.

While I believe a firm's reputation is the result of the collective reputations of its people, it's important to foster a culture of knowledge sharing rather than knowledge hoarding. The old adage, "knowledge is power," is certainly true in professional services firms. Industry expertise housed in the minds of your firm's industry thought leaders needs to evolve to industry expertise shared across the firm. Not every professional will build their industry specialty and focus only on clients in one industry. Many will remain generalists that service clients across multiple industries. A firm is highly advised to ensure these generalists know when to include colleagues with the right industry expertise in their client interactions and client pursuits.

As the discipline and methodology that optimizes knowledge sharing across the firm, KM strategies benefit all aspects of the firm's work. But KM is especially valuable when building a strong industry specialization strategy.

Here are some key elements and advantages of a firm-wide KM system:

- The company's intranet is the primary knowledge-sharing platform for most professional services firms. Once a firm becomes larger than one or two offices in nearby geographies, the intranet is essential for efficiently sharing knowledge across the entire firm.

- All employees should have access to the same up-to-date, approved versions of essential documents and work papers to help them do their work accurately and efficiently.

- Creating a "one-firm" mentality or culture is enhanced when all employees have easy access to the same internal messaging.

- Promoting the firm's desired business culture is easier and more effective using internal communications enabled by a firm-wide intranet platform.

Industry groups, in particular, derive huge benefits by maintaining and using the firm's intranet platform. Each industry group should have its own industry web pages on the firm's intranet so it can easily share the following types of information, within their group and across the firm:

- **Industry knowledge.** Each industry group openly but safely shares its content to help team members continually improve their industry knowledge – ranging from foundational information about industry business models, industry players and financial drivers, to continually updated industry trends and economic factors that impact industry clients and prospects.

- **Sales and presentation materials.** Marketing collateral, proposals or standard proposals, pitch presentations and other marketing tools can be easily accessible to all on the intranet platform.

- **Deliverables and work papers.** Relevant industry-focused work papers, templates, engagement letters and even best-in-class engagement deliverables should be shared on each industry portal. This ensures consistent service methodologies and deliverables across the firm for similar engagements. It also increases efficiency, since professionals can access approved versions of content or methodologies and don't have to recreate the wheel by starting from scratch.

Summing It Up

A serious investment in developing an industry learning strategy is an essential element of a well-rounded and effective industry program. Since every industry is different, and the knowledge or course content is housed within your firm's subject matter experts, these professionals will need to contribute to the development of courses and curriculum. Many firms employ in-house learning and development resources or they outsource this function. The curriculum and course development for each industry group should be a collaborative effort between the industry subject matter experts and the continuing professional education team. Your industry teams can seek out relevant course content that can be purchased from industry trade or professional associations, which can minimize the time your client-serving professionals might need to contribute to industry course development.

One way every firm can help their professionals learn about their chosen industry most efficiently and productively is by using knowledge management tools and methods to share industry expertise across their offices, their service line departments, and their industry groups. An online platform for a well-managed intranet, the internal enterprise-wide tool is the way to expedite knowledge sharing and promoting easy access to knowledge and informal learning opportunities for each industry team.

8.

Think of Each Industry as a Close-Knit Community

Each industry market is a close-knit community, making it easy to find direction and focus when building your network and reputation as an industry specialist.

Here's why industry specialization is a surefire way to use your time in the marketplace efficiently, productively, and successfully.

- You want to fish where the fish are.

- Each industry community has its own pond, or, community, where you find the key players, the micro-environment, the micro-financial and economic factors. You'll also find all your competitors fishing for their next client in the same pond.

Your firm and professionals will want to stake out your territory, where you become a known quantity, build trusting relationships, and demonstrate your own expertise – your corner of that big pond.

For example, if your target market is attorneys for litigation support, you want to network with lawyers where you can find them – perhaps in the real estate section of the state bar association where you become a speaker or a known quantity in this small community.

Taken to the next level, an even narrower focus is an approach proven to be extremely successful for some. Become a big fish in a little pond, rather than another little fish in the ocean! If you're one of just three national experts in a narrow niche industry or market – let's say, fisheries, or dairies – while the market is certainly small, it has the advantage of being very well defined, like a small community where everyone knows everyone else. You can become the "go-to" preferred valuation specialist in this small community. There is much less competition, and very soon you will have almost cornered the market.

Each industry community has its own pond, or, community, where you find the key players, the micro-environment, the micro-financial and economic factors.....Your firm and professionals will want to stake out your territory, where you become a known quantity, build trusting relationships, and demonstrate your own expertise – your corner of that big pond.

If the community is nursing homes, then the different players in this industry are the nursing home owners, their CFOs or controllers, and the bankers and lawyers who also thrive in this specific marketplace or community. It includes the ancillary services in the healthcare industry that may also target nursing homes to provide services, such as contract therapy services, pharmacies, medical van transportation providers, medical equipment providers, and many more.

If the community is supermarkets, then the different fish – the players in your focus community – are food processors and distributors, store fixture providers, grocery retail software providers, food equipment purveyors, and of course, the bankers and lawyers who contribute to sustaining the supermarket sector of the food and beverage industry. The network you can explore is this entire universe (or community) of relevant players to build relationships with and channels of distribution where you can market your service expertise.

Your firm's marketing resources, whether in-house or from an outsourced marketing consultant, are responsible for supporting each aspiring Industry Luminary and the industry teams to best leverage these industry venues where industry decision makers and influencers can regularly be found. The marketers guide the industry team members with the following strategic decisions:

- Marketers should research and select which industry trade associations the industry team will focus on to build their presence and reputation. Industries often have multiple trade associations with national organizations and state chapters. There are conferences with speaking opportunities, planning committees where the real work of the organizations gets done, and learning programs that showcase Industry Luminaries sharing their expertise. Your marketer's responsibility is to recommend the best trade association(s) where your future Industry Luminaries should invest their time and the firm's money.

- Once certain trade associations are targeted, the marketer needs to share a calendar of the selected association events where your industry teams will need to build their network and their reputations. Speaking slots are often "pay to play," requiring certain levels of sponsorship by the firm to guarantee a certain number of speaking opportunities. Your industry team's presence, in the form of a booth at a conference or tables reserved at dinner events, will yield greater exposure and opportunities to showcase your professionals' industry insights to enhance their reputation and familiarity with the target market.

- Marketing should leverage your industry teams' thought leadership content. Most industries have a range of media that the industry community reads on a regular basis. These publications, whether digital or hard copy, present opportunities to place your future Industry Luminary's insightful articles, blogs, quotes, interviews, podcasts, or webcasts in front of the eyes or ears of your target audience.

- The marketer should partner with the industry team to develop an annual calendar of events for networking, speaking slots, and thought leadership content placement where every team member is a contributor in ways that best fit their strengths, as networkers, as public speakers and as authors of written or oral thought leadership. While acting as contributors, the industry team members are also investing in themselves, as their personal reputations as industry thought leaders are established and strengthened.

Industry Players Form a Tight-Knit Community

Viewing industries as close-knit communities makes it easy to find direction and focus when building industry networks and reputations as industry specialists.

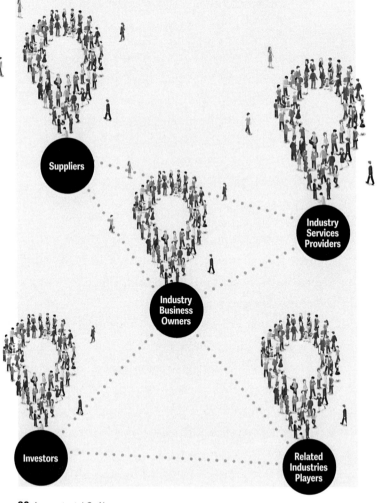

 **Reality Check**

Marketing is a profession too!

Since marketing is critical to the success of your firm's industry practice groups, it's important to understand the value professional marketers bring to the table.

In smaller firms, I've seen marketing departments populated with self-made, homegrown marketers who were promoted from receptionist to administrative assistant, marketing coordinator and beyond. Consequently, they often receive little respect and are treated like order takers, incapable of building a marketing strategy, which is an essential element of a strong business growth plan for each industry practice group. Not that it's impossible for a great marketing resource to be developed in-house, but marketing is a discipline with proven methodologies taught in undergraduate and graduate school programs, very similar to the programs that produce accounting professionals.

In environments where marketing team members don't get (or deserve) respect as sophisticated marketing professionals, accounting and tax professionals often decide to develop their own marketing strategies and just have marketers act as the "doers" or task-takers, not the thinkers. While expert in their fields, accounting professionals are rarely, if ever, trained and experienced in the marketing discipline! The unfortunate result of expecting accounting professionals to perform the marketing function is typically a suboptimal marketing strategic plan. Worse, the time and money the firm invests in executing marketing tactics will yield a suboptimal ROI. Without marketing professionals, the firm is working with one hand tied behind its back, and its industry program strategy will not be fully leveraged to assist in the firm's overall growth and the growth of individual professionals.

As professional services firms grow, they need true professional marketing expertise. So, while it may be tempting, it's best not to rely on expert accountants or tax gurus to serve as the marketing think tank. The investment in wise counsel from marketing specialists will be well spent when combined with the business plan to build the firm's reputation around selected industries. If employing professional marketers is outside the budget, start with part-time or outsourced marketing consultants to provide the strategic marketing advice you need.

Summing It Up

We all know that close-knit communities tend to congregate in their regular hangouts, enjoy the same kind of entertainment, share successes and problems, and trade tips on how to get ahead. All this camaraderie and conversation happens in the confines of each industry's close-knit community. These industry communities include a set of well-known industry players. There are known industry leaders, as well as a cadre of start-ups at the other end of the spectrum. There are lawyers, bankers and software vendors that are uniquely dedicated to each industry community.

This industry community model is the magic bullet that makes networking and building a reputation as an industry thought leader so compelling for you and your firm's professionals.

Your firm's marketing team, whether in-house or outsourced, should be aware of the marketplace venues and culture for each industry your firm is trying to penetrate. The natural partnership between your industry experts and the supporting marketing resource is needed to develop and execute an effective industry marketing plan.

9.

An Outstanding Client Experience Drives the Firm of the Future

Defining your firm's client experience (CX) and actualizing that experience consistently across the firm is a golden ticket to building a Firm of the Future. A Firm of the Future not only survives but thrives because it has capitalized on the fast-paced changes impacting the accounting and consulting industry, such as artificial intelligence, machine learning and robotic process automation. In this chapter, you'll discover exactly what is meant by a "client experience strategy" and how it applies to a professional services firm. I also reveal some of the secrets of building a successful CX initiative, so you can begin your own initiative at your firm.

Right after industry knowledge and experience, delivering a better client experience is the next competitive differentiator accounting and professional services firms are addressing. Very soon, for many clients, it won't be enough to receive top-quality technical expertise and proficient deliverables. In today's competitive business environment, clients are learning to expect a consistently better experience from trusted service providers. Professional services firms looking to grow at rates faster than their competition are developing "service experiences" that make them stand out from the pack.

There was a time when delivering a quality product or service for an agreed-upon fee was all clients expected. But today, that's not enough. Clients want and expect a deeper, richer relationship from their accounting professional – they want a business partner. They want an experience that feels customized to them.

Very soon, for many clients, it won't be enough to receive top-quality technical expertise and proficient deliverables. In today's competitive business environment, clients are learning to expect a consistently better experience from trusted service providers. Professional services firms looking to grow at rates faster than their competition are developing "service experiences" that make them stand out from the pack.

Client experience is the sum of the interactions or all the various touches a client has with your firm. Their perception of the value you bring develops from those interactions.

All parties who engage with your firm for paid services, regardless of the amount or type of service, can report on the "client experience" they received. The CX journey begins the moment you start building a relationship and a client decides to select your firm for the engagement. It continues throughout the engagement process and the delivery of the completed services, any touchpoints after or outside the engagement period, and, ultimately, through their decision to either continue or renew the engagement, expand the relationship with additional services, or terminate the engagement relationship altogether. This client journey can be mapped out, dissected, and assessed to determine how the firm might improve any of the touchpoints along the way.

A typical firm that hasn't prioritized the development of a client experience initiative will often face the following problems:

- No national, unified client experience. The firm's acquisition strategy may have resulted in different cultures, history and approaches in different geographic regions.

- Differentiation is difficult. A regionally organized firm will have different industries of strength in each region. These firms can find it difficult to articulate a unique value proposition.

- Cross-selling doesn't occur naturally. Due to the diversity, breadth and size of the firm, cross-selling is challenging. Furthermore, the firm's compensation and awards structures do not encourage cross-selling.

- The firm can't respond to client issues because they lack visibility into them. There are no customer service standards or recovery practices currently in place.

- Firms often don't track client attrition or understand why clients leave. Of course, if this understanding isn't addressed, no actions will be taken to improve the situation.

A strong CX program needs to be a part of the firm's larger picture – a clear mission and vision should be consistent with the firm's brand.

- Core values, like teamwork, passion, and innovation
- A clear firm mission, such as, "Understand our clients and provide services to help them achieve their business and financial goals."
- Vision: Be the firm of choice for clients and the professionals who serve them.
- Strategy: A unified client experience delivered consistently.
- Brand examples:
    - Deloitte – The firm where the best want to be
    - RSM - The power of being understood
    - Marcum - Ask Marcum - The people who have all the answers get their answers from Marcum

Your firm's CX strategy should be built using a model that leverages three components:

1. Voice of the client
2. CX skills and resources
3. Industry-based client teams

The Voice of the Client *(aka Client Feedback)*

When launching your firm's CX program, client feedback (also known as "the voice of the client") is of primary importance. Below are the basic steps or phases to build out a "voice of the client" initiative:

- **Conduct a baseline client survey** and analyze your results.

- **Roll out the CX strategy** at a partner retreat or other firmwide venue.

- **Launch a pilot Voice of the Client program** in one region or office and begin to gather client data *on an ongoing basis,* and adjust your plan based on findings.

- **Expand the client feedback program to the entire firm**, region by region or office by office.

CX Skills and Resources

The CX strategy will only be successful if every employee is all in. Everyone counts. Everyone in the firm contributes to its success, as everyone has a relentless focus on the clients. Therefore, an important element of the CX strategy is a "skills and resources" plan to raise awareness and educate the firm about the elements of client experience. This plan includes the following steps:

- **Create a CX working group** and refine the client journey.

- **Design CX training** in coordination with your firm's learning organization and CX training across all existing soft-skill learning programs, such as executive leadership training, new manager training and trusted consulting programs.

Elements of a Client Experience and the Client Journey

"Client Experience" is an all-encompassing client-centric model.

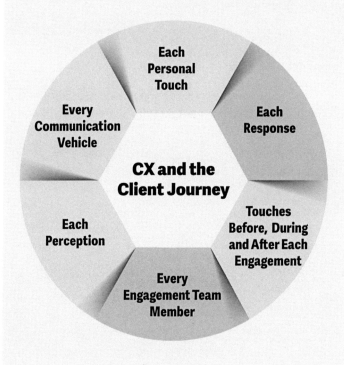

- **Establish a CX intranet presence** on the firm's intranet platform. These internal web pages will include resources and tools, definitions of client service standards, client journey mapping, minor and major interactions, and client focus resources.

Elements of a client experience initiative include:

- Vision and strategy
- Client feedback
- Training
- Common service methodology and resources
- Performance management and compensation
- Brand integration
- Internal communications
- Metrics
- Sales integration
- Technology & reporting
- Product development

All this information about client experience strategies can be overwhelming and the investment difficult to justify to managers of smaller firms. But client experience excellence can and should be designed and achievable for firms of every size.

Therefore, a client experience plan should be rightsized

and customized for your firm. Starting with a baseline client feedback survey can help you understand where your firm stands in your client's eyes. Client surveys can uncover both what your firm does well and where your energy should be invested to improve any weaknesses revealed. Design the client experience plan that is within your firm's budget and the capabilities and bandwidth available inside of the firm to work with external expertise. Client experience plans can grow as the firm develops, as long as you establish achievable goals. Client experience champions should identify low-hanging fruit, or areas where improving aspects of your clients' experience will be manageable and appreciated by them.

> *Starting with a baseline client feedback survey can help you understand where your firm stands in your client's eyes. Client surveys can uncover both what your firm does well and where your energy should be invested to improve any weaknesses revealed.*

Industry-based client teams for superior client experience

Forming industry-based client teams enables your team to view the client holistically. The team is empowered to perceive the totality of the client's needs and how the depth and breadth of the firm can be brought to bear to help that client face its business challenges and opportunities. This approach demonstrates that it's less important to define the client as an audit or tax client, but rather as a real estate client or a healthcare client, first and foremost. When the right industry expertise is included on the client's team, the most relevant services will be offered to meet the client's needs.

 **Reality Check**

Building trust between partners and encouraging "firm-first" and "client-first" behaviors can supercharge growth.

My experience across firms of all sizes validates the importance of trust and sharing among partners and leaders. I've also repeatedly witnessed the natural friction that occurs in a firm culture that, on the one hand, fosters entrepreneurship and on the other encourages trust and sharing. An equal dose of "eat what you kill" and firm-first or client-first behaviors is necessary for most firms to achieve growth. This is especially true for industry practice groups that span geographies and service lines.

The beauty of industry practice groups is that members come from the assurance, tax and consulting (or advisory) service lines. The ideal industry team facilitates the breakdown of the silos created by traditionally separate service lines or functions, where the assurance or audit engagement team is one team and the tax engagement team is a separate functional team. For every industry group, the goal is to view each client holistically, so the relationship partners have a deep understanding of the client's business challenges and goals in the context of their industry and their competition. The relationship partner's job is to provide the client with any of the firm's professional services that support and enable the client to achieve its business goals. This necessitates comprehensive knowledge of the firm's full depth and breadth of technical expertise. Not only is the relationship partner an audit or tax professional, but he or she is an ambassador for the full gamut of the firm's advisory services.

But knowledge of the firm's full suite of services isn't enough! The relationship partner needs to know and trust the partners who will deliver these specialty services the client so desperately needs. The relationship partner must share this client (and, thereby, risk the client relationship) with other partners that he/she doesn't work with closely or regularly. The relationship partner may not fully understand the expertise and specialty services the colleague can provide, nor the qualities and intricacies of the engagement deliverable the colleague's team will produce.

Typically, the audit partner's engagement with a client is recurring work, repeating and perhaps expanding upon the audit engagement year after year. The first year is often significantly less profitable for the audit engagement team, but the team is counting on many years of continuing engagements, when greater realization is often achieved. It's hard for the audit partner to risk his client relationship on a consulting or tax specialty engagement, which can often be a "one-and-done" project, with no expectation of follow-on or recurring engagements.

Also, due to independence restrictions, it's common for a firm to be required to choose to either pursue the audit engagement, which may be recurring, or instead, pursue a much more lucrative specialty advisory service engagement, which has no promise of future engagements or recurring fees once the project is done.

Yet, time and again, it's been proven that the future growth of most accounting, tax and advisory firms depends on the advisory services side of the house. Audit and tax work has become more and more automated, with repetitive work often shipped offshore at lower cost. These economic and technological realities drive down fees and commoditize many firms' standard audit and tax compliance engagements. In addition, many specialty services can or should be customized to meet the unique needs of businesses in specific industries. These industry-based services can be bundled and productized, resulting in highly differentiated products that can command healthy margins and long-term client relationships.

Changing the mindset to "firm first" and "client first," rather than "me first"

Still, many partners and leaders find they are uncomfortable cross-selling or going beyond selling their own expertise to selling the services of their industry practice group colleagues. Getting partners to think beyond their own world of tax or audit requires the blinders to be removed and minds to be opened to think: "What's good for the client? How can our whole firm service this client best? What expertise in our firm should I bring to the table so our client and our firm will be most successful?"

What's needed to change your partners' mindsets to think "firm first" and "client first"? Your challenge is to do the following:

- **Prioritize and allocate time** to build camaraderie and trust between partners across service lines and geographies, focusing on giving industry groups the time and space to bond.

Building industry focus and an outstanding client experience is an *intertwined process*

Defining your firm's client experience and delivering it consistently across the firm is a golden ticket to becoming a true Firm of the Future.

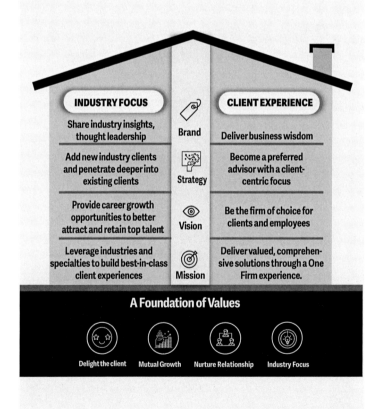

Chapter 9: An Outstanding Client Experience Drives the Firm of the Future

- **Realign financial incentives and public recognition** to match achievable growth goals through cross-selling rather than allowing partners to sell just one service line – their own.

- **Identify bad behaviors and call them out!** I don't mean public castigation, but rather private and very clear messages to put an end to behaviors that undermine firm-wide growth goals. Old behaviors can reinforce counterproductive silos, rather than what's best for the client. If allowed to continue unchecked, the old-school partners who are resistant to change will frustrate and thwart your firm's investment in a forward-thinking strategy for sustainable and accelerated growth!

Summing It Up

Client experience programs have well-established measurable ROI enjoyed by firms that have invested in these client-centric models. You and your firm may be considering a client experience plan to deepen client relationships and create value above and beyond the services your firm provides. Your firm can develop a well-rounded but rightsized client experience plan that will help you achieve these goals.

10.

Industry Program + Client Experience Strategy = Accelerated Growth

Going to market by industry strongly reinforces the principles of an equally strong client experience (CX) strategy and vice versa. These two strategies or programs are strongly complementary.

Industry groups should address the CX strategy relevant to each group's client base, but this should be done consistently across all industries and across the firm.

- **Roll out** a CX program to each industry team.
- **Conduct client segmentation** and key account programs within each industry team, region by region.
- **Design the elements of a successful CX for each tier or segment** in the context of each industry.
- **Reinforce CX training and resources** for each industry team.

Client segmentation within each industry drives the levels of the client experience

A key element of CX is client segmentation or tiering of clients. The segmentation process helps to identify the firm's most treasured clients and why they are so treasured. The first step in discovery is to determine which client attributes make these clients eligible for the top category – the most treasured clients of the firm. Perhaps the "top 100" clients of the firm are in that category because of a mixture of the following client attributes:

- These clients generate the highest fees. These high fees could be due to the size and complexity of the client's business or the fact that your firm is deeply embedded in this client because you already provide it with multiple services, or both!

- Client tenure – these are the clients who have been with the firm the longest.

- Client size – regardless of fees, these clients are the largest companies by revenue that the firm serves.

- Client fits into the firm's sweet spot. Management should determine the firm's revenue range sweet spot. If they currently serve clients that are $10 million to $50 million in revenues, the firm's leaders may see the potential for growth if it can aim higher, say at clients that are $25 million to $100 million in revenue. These larger companies will have larger wallet share, i.e., the appetite to spend money on discretionary services. These noncompliance-related services aren't required to stay in business (like filing a tax return, which is required by law), but management can opt into these specialty services if they're convinced of the value-add the services will bring to their business.

- Client penetration – the number of services the firm provides to the client is a measure of how deeply the firm penetrates, reinforcing its relationship with the client.

- Client aligns with the firm's areas of industry expertise, therefore allowing the firm to provide industry insights and knowledge the client will value.

Top-tier clients receive the white-glove client experience.
Often, firms' data analytics reveal that at least 80 percent of their revenue is derived from 20 percent of their clients. Many firms uncover the fact that upward of 90 percent of revenue is attributable to only 10 percent of their clients. While those treasured Tier 1 clients are extremely important to the firm, in fact, their importance puts the firm at risk. That's because losing just one of those clients could have a devastatingly negative impact on the firm. Considering exactly what kind of "white-glove" client experience should be designed and delivered to this top-tier client group is thus a crucial element of a successful client experience program.

Tier 2 clients receive a highly a customized CX bundle of value-add services.
Firms often discover that the second tier of clients (those with the potential to become Tier 1 clients) is the most important tier of all. That's because this client group is comprised of clients that have the potential to buy a variety of services, which allows the service provider to deepen its relationship with the company's decision makers. Ultimately, they represent the

greatest opportunity to grow the firm's overall revenue across services. The client experience team will determine what level of investment in the cultivation of these Tier 2 client relationships should deliver the reward of moving them up to Tier 1.

Tier 3 clients should receive a defined CX package that supports and monitors the growth of these emerging companies.
Clients in Tier 3 could be considered dynamic clients, because they are moving. This tier includes many start-ups that are small today but could be growing aggressively. Many start-up or very small clients fit into this category. Today, the fees they generate are relatively small, and they may not have wallet share that allows them to purchase discretionary services. Many of these clients will fail, close, or simply always stay small. But the minority that thrive and grow present a great opportunity for your firm to grow the relationship over time. It's very hard to know which small clients will fail or stagnate and which will take off and fly to high heights, and there could be risk in the choices your firm makes. At the very least, your firm should monitor these clients' growth and financial viability over a limited number of years so it can regularly reassess the value of keeping these companies as long-term clients. The level of client experience should be established and delivered consistently for this tier as well.

Tier 4 clients are typically local office clients.
This lowest tier of clients may be the bread and butter of local offices. Local offices may view many of these clients as profitable, even though they are small and their fees are also small. Each partner, each practice group, and each office should take

a close look at their lowest-fee clients and determine which clients are important enough to keep. The firm's growth strategy, for example, may include a vision to go upstream to target larger companies. To achieve this vision, the strategy must include not only what steps the firm will take, but also what the firm will *not* do. Achieving the vision of "going upstream" means saying "no" to some clients or future clients when they are off-strategy. Once the clients that should be shed are identified, a large group of small clients that still need baseline service and baseline client experience will always remain. Firm leadership needs to determine what the baseline level of client experience means and ensure it is delivered consistently. The CX work group determines the standardized baseline level of value-add touches and experiences that shape the client journey for every single Tier 4 client.

> *Each partner, each practice group, and each office should take a close look at their lowest-fee clients and determine whch clients are important enough to keep.... Achieving the vision of "going upstream" means saying "no" to some clients or future clients when they are off-strategy.*

Client segments might look like this, for example:

- Tier 1, your treasured clients, are the most important clients of the firm (i.e., top 100 clients).
- Tier 2, your high-impact clients, have potential to become treasured clients.

Client Segmentation Drives Industry Enhanced Client Experience

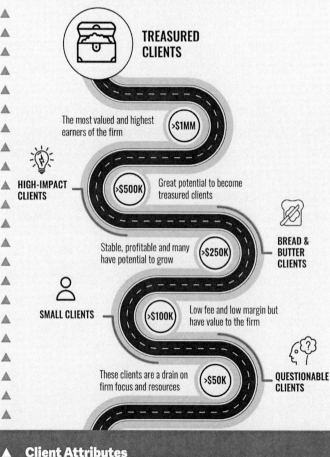

- **Client Attributes**
- **Fees** – Higher fees and higher margins
- **Tenure** – Years as a client
- **Services** – Multiple, deeper penetration
- **Revenue Band or AUM** – Client size and potential wallet share

- Tier 3 clients are the bread and butter of your local offices (profitable, recurring fees).

- Tier 4 clients are small companies or small-fee clients, but they're important to your local offices. You likely have many clients generating very low-fee and/or low-margin engagements.

- Tier 5 clients are "questionable clients." These clients are a drain on your firm's focus and resources. Most successful firms need to periodically go through a client-culling process. Some partners find it hard to cull their clients because it's hard to say no, or to give up a client. If this is a problem for you or your firm, it's important to openly address this topic with your managing and line partners.

Is your industry focus too broad or too narrow?

Another aspect of the client's attributes to be considered when tiering and targeting for client experience excellence is determining when your areas of industry expertise should drill down deeper from the level of the umbrella industry to the level of sectors or even subsectors. For example, should your firm develop or support a very narrow niche within an industry, such as banks, or serve clients across the spectrum of a larger industry umbrella, such as financial services? Of course, the narrower the niches you serve, the greater your focus on a specific target, but then you are placing your bets on a few narrower areas of focus rather than broader industry buckets. Depending on the expertise that resides in your firm, these strategic decisions will vary from industry to industry.

 **Reality Check**

Industry vs. sector, or *"A rose by any other name would smell as sweet."*

The words used within your firm can significantly affect the business culture and the success of an industry strategy. When I was working for a Big Four firm, I observed that they grappled with the "industry" vs. "sector" question as its industry program matured. Ultimately, they elected to focus on "a few" industries and a limited number of "sectors" within each industry. The industries were proclaimed to be administrative umbrellas that housed the related sectors. Sectors, such as restaurants, within the food and beverage industry, allowed the practice to drill down to the next level, narrowing down to focus on our clients' specific competitive marketplace. The firm determined which sectors held the highest growth potential and which industry grouping made sense for that sector. Sector leaders were assigned greater importance than industry leaders. These umbrella industry leaders played an administrative role, and, often, one of the sector leaders doubled as the industry leader. For example, the banking sector leader also led the umbrella financial services industry.

In this industry example, real estate was no longer an industry but a sector within the financial services umbrella industry, along with the insurance, banking and asset management sectors. Due to the convergence of industries in the marketplace, clients can cross over or span two industries, which naturally leads to collaboration across sectors underneath the financial services industry umbrella. For example, real estate funds are targets or clients of the real estate industry practice. Large insurance companies have very substantial investment portfolios, which include investments in real estate funds with real estate managers who oversee these real estate assets. The partners in the insurance industry practice were well positioned to make introductions between their real estate practice colleagues and their insurance company clients. As the real estate industry practice senior manager, part of my job at the Big Four firm was to identify those synergies and facilitate collaboration between professionals focused on the different sectors.

Prioritizing industries and sectors based on the firm's growth expectations was a careful and delicate responsibility of the firm's leadership. The priority growth industries and sectors were destined to receive larger financial investments in the form of marketing budgets and expanded internal resources.

Intentionally differentiating "industries" from "sectors" and clarifying the difference between the traditional industry practice groups and other firm strategies for growth is essential. One Big Four firm coined the term "IMOs" or "integrated market offerings" to distinguish these cross-functional practice groups from industry and sector specialty teams.

One IMO was a merger and acquisition (M&A) business-building strategy that offered an array of services to private equity funds targeting operating businesses in which to invest and companies that want to get "sell-ready" because they need an investor to capitalize or monetize the business. Bundling services from due diligence to deal close to post-merger integration is a robust growth strategy, but it's not an industry-specific strategy. This M&A IMO targeted clients across industries, not just those in one specific industry. In very large firms with many M&A professionals, they can split up "by industry" and create sub-teams that not only offer the transaction advisory services, but also industry-specific expertise.

That strategy can still work in smaller firms if you designate groups of professionals to cover just two or three, rather than all, industries in this area of technical specialty. The SEC practice also spans industries, representing another IMO focused on the technical audit skills needed to assist companies in "going public" and meeting the ongoing SEC financial reporting requirements.

For smaller firms with high-growth specialty service offerings that span industries, there is an obvious solution. Although professionals with specialty service expertise are "generalists" across industries, they should be expected or required to bring the relevant industry expert to the pursuit team. This deep industry expert should work with the engagement team, at least during that team's planning sessions, where the team reviews the client holistically for cross-selling opportunities.

Summing It Up

The best of both worlds, industry specialization and outstanding client experience, gets even better when these two strategies work in concert. You can't successfully have one without the other. Industry subject matter experts must use that expertise to benefit clients, so they can be treated to client experience excellence. A client-centric plan in the current economic environment is less about building personal relationships and more about offering clients relevant expertise that they value to help them achieve their business goals.

Attempting to build meaningful and deeper client relationships without demonstrating your strong knowledge of the client's business in the context of their industry is analogous to the emperor having no clothes. The client who is deeply entrenched and invested in his/her business can quickly discern if you are truly knowledgeable about their industry and have meaningful insights to share. You just can't fake it and hope that your caring personality will win you a loyal client.

11.

Become a Recognized Industry Luminary

Now that your firm is becoming a *known* industry thought leader in the specific industries your firm's management team chooses, business owners and managers in these industries will be looking to you to help them achieve their business goals. Your brand and reputation in each industry's marketplace will be uniquely entrenched. Clients and prospects will recognize your company as the "go-to firm" where they can not only get professional services for a fee, but also find a service provider with deep industry knowledge that can add real value for them and their business.

Leverage and encourage *industry expertise* to create new and expand existing client relationships.

- Build a national reputation for deep industry expertise.
- Become thought leaders and go-to experts.
- Deliver value over competitors and drive profitable growth.
- Develop a "no coasting" mentality across the firm – everyone contributes to growth.

Below are five ways to become an Industry Luminary, to

accelerate growth for each individual professional and for the firm:

- **Be the thin edge of the wedge.** Select a new or innovative niche, if possible – become an early adopter.

- **Be the emperor who *has* clothes.** It can't just be about building relationships; it has to be about offering real and relevant expertise.

- **Integrate industry expertise with a technical specialty.** Join two areas of expertise. You can be a specialty tax expert, or you can be a construction expert. But you can further differentiate yourself if you are a construction expert with specialty tax expertise relevant to your construction clients and targets.

- **Narrow your focus.** Most firms have large umbrella industries, like consumer products or manufacturing and distribution. Your firm and professionals can stake out a niche in a narrow space, such as metal processors or craft breweries, for example. Be a bigger fish in a smaller pond. You'll stand out in a much smaller crowd.

- **Curate, curate, curate.** Clients have lots of sources of industry knowledge, but you can become their curator of information and news. One way of becoming their trusted industry advisor is to offer only the best thinking and, in particular, your firm's point of view.

# Reality Check

Be a blowfish and use the game-changer strategy.

Even the largest firms with seemingly unlimited resources must make choices about where best to invest. Having to choose can lead to creativity and innovation, and much smaller organizations can learn from larger firms' experience and borrow from the same playbook. Along the way, I learned the biggest firms make use of the "blowfish" and "game-changer" strategies. Your firm can also be a blowfish and recruit some industry game changers.

What's a blowfish and why would my firm want to be one? A blowfish is a little fish that can puff itself up many times its true size. By puffing up with air, the little blowfish exhibits a much larger, more important presence and faces its foes with apparent size and strength.

Be a blowfish! Big firms with relatively small industry practices, or much smaller firms with small niche practices, are all trying to achieve similar goals. They both want to impress the marketplace with deep and insightful industry expertise that will be valued by potential clients in that space. If your firm's practice in an industry is just emerging and you're in the process of developing young talent, or perhaps the practice is limited to a few strong professionals, becoming a blowfish could be an effective strategy.

Showcase your industry depth while you are still building it

How exactly can your firm's industry group present itself as the very strong practice it aspires to become? How can you become the blowfish? Becoming a blowfish is accomplished with game changers! Okay, you say, what's a game changer?

Your firm may be able to identify and recruit one of these well-respected thought leaders who can help boost your industry practice group's reputation, well before your industry practice group's accounting, tax or advisory service professionals have built their own reputations as thought leaders.

Within every industry is small cadre of game changers. These are the seasoned, well-known idols, celebrities or elders in their field. These are men and women who built their careers and sometimes their wealth through their industry's school of hard knocks. They've built successful businesses or professional careers and become known as industry titans or gurus. At the top of their game, they became industry or professional thought leaders, working on advisory boards, directing industry associations, or becoming authors and speakers recognized and respected for their wisdom in their fields. Your firm may be able to identify and recruit one of these well-respected thought leaders who can help boost your industry practice group's reputation, well before your industry practice group's accounting, tax or advisory service professionals have built their own reputations as thought leaders.

Many of these seasoned, publicly admired industry leaders are surprisingly available as they wind down their business or professional activities and transition to a less frenetic work lifestyle. Similarly, you can find industry experts, who can be prolific thought leaders, from the ranks of professionals who spent decades as financial investment company industry analysts. For example, a food and beverage industry analyst or apparel and consumer products industry analyst could head to a second career as your firm's industry thought leader.

How much will it cost? It will cost a lot less than the alternative! Your new industry practice will require the investment of time – it will take years of building the practice and reputation of your line partners who are gradually becoming respected industry thought leaders. Your practice will also require the investment of the alternative use of your partners' time – sacrificing billable time serving clients, as, instead, they spend their time in the marketplace as speakers, writers and webcast or podcast presenters. Don't get me wrong. You still need your partners to continually build their industry reputations. But most firms can't afford to have even the most promising marketplace thought leaders completely give up client work and stop billing for services in order to become industry thought leaders. Most partners are expected to manage a difficult balancing act, juggling line partner responsibilities and time-consuming market-facing thought leadership activities.

Your firm has a good shot at acquiring a proven industry thought leader as a part-time contract freelancer. This industry guru, known and respected, can become your firm's "Joe Smith, Chairman of the Center for Excellence for the Construction Industry." Or "Jane Adams, Leader of the Healthcare Institute of Innovation" or "John Jay, Banking Industry Thought Leader." Your arrangement with your part-time thought leader can include: 1) Authoring regular articles for your firm's website or industry newsletter,

Be a Blowfish!

Present yourself and your firm as BIG in your chosen industries.

2) Participating in pursuit team meetings with industry targets, 3) Participating in meetings with your firm's most important industry clients, and 4) Speaking or presenting at your firm's sponsored industry conferences or webcasts.

The dollars you spend on "game changers" will be some of the best investments you can make to pump up your firm's reputation in its chosen industries, and ultimately its revenues, since industry players gravitate to service providers recognized as dedicated thought leaders and advisors to their specific industry community.

Play big, like a blowfish!

Summing It Up

Accounting, tax and advisory firms are increasing revenues and profitability when they go narrow. However, the deep industry expertise housed within the firm needs to become well known outside the firm, where the industry marketplace is analogous to a close-knit community. There are great marketing strategies that will allow your firm to play big in the specific industry markets you choose. You can stand out above the rest, even as you are just nurturing your rising stars into becoming the industry thought leaders of tomorrow. Your firm can be like a blowfish, presenting a strong image by affiliating with a low-cost, high-ROI Industry Luminary.

12.

Get Going!

There will never be a better time than right now to focus on developing strategies to achieve extraordinary and sustainable growth. If you're interested in the contents of this book, your organization is poised and motivated to achieve extraordinary growth, both for your professionals' personal careers and for the firm.

Here are three things your firm can do right now to get started on achieving that growth. These three steps apply to each professional and to your entire organization.

- **Be focused.** Choose an industry specialty(ies) or recommit to ones you've already chosen.

- **Have a plan.** Write down your personal marketing plan and share it with your team. Writing things down is motivating, because it makes your dreams concrete. Research shows that if you don't write them down, you're much less likely to achieve your dreams.

- **Be consistent.** You're in this for the long haul. A one-week or one-month push isn't enough to achieve long-lasting results.

 Reality Check

My personal message to you

If you are reading this book, you probably work at an accounting or consulting firm, and you are interested in industry specialization or enhancing client experience to jump-start your firm's revenue growth. If your firm is already known for its depth and expertise in your chosen industries, that's great! Maybe you or someone in your firm already has deep industry expertise, but that expertise isn't converting to winning more clients or being recognized by your existing clients as a differentiator they see as your edge over the competition. Maybe this industry focus just isn't resulting in greater revenue or "stickier" clients for your firm! It may feel like your industry leaders or practice groups aren't equipped to win in the marketplace and they are spinning their wheels and wasting otherwise billable time. This is probably disappointing and frustrating.

Or, maybe you're just beginning (or partway down the road) to build your firm's reputation as the go-to firm in specific industries. It's likely many of the partners in your firm have lots of experience serving businesses across many different industries. But nobody, and no firm, becomes famous by being a generalist! It can be challenging to change people's mindsets mid-career, by asking them to move from being a generalist to being a specialist. Compounding your problem is that your firm's young rising stars need coaching and role models to develop their own deep industry expertise. If your partners are mostly generalists, it's hard to find leaders inside the firm who can motivate and champion industry specialization. To sum it up, changing from a firm of generalists to a firm known for its industry specialties is an uphill challenge.

I can help your firm achieve accelerated revenue growth and gain a competitive advantage with the most efficient and productive use of your professionals' time and energy. At the same time, we are creating a fulfilling and engaging career path for you and your colleagues by fueling your passions in the market sectors you choose to focus on.

With my expertise I can help you build, launch, and execute an industry strategy or client experience plan that is right for you and your firm, so you can turbocharge growth and achieve extraordinary ROI for the investments you make in yourself, your professionals, and your firm.

If your firm is feeding the pipeline with new clients, but at the same time losing clients who jump ship because they can get the work done more cheaply by your low-fee competitor, it may feel like you are working hard but just treading water. You may have thought about designing a "client experience program" where getting client feedback and creating client service standards of excellence can start solving this problem. If you are considering the advantages of a client experience strategy aimed at deepening client relationships and creating value above and beyond the service your firm provides, a comprehensive, but rightsized program will help you achieve those goals.

I've been in professional services my entire career. For the last 20 years, I've worked at a Big Four firm and three other top 20 national accounting and advisory firms where I focused on growing revenues and clients through industry expertise and client experience excellence. I've partnered with leadership to design and execute growth strategies tailored to the needs of their firms.

With my expertise I can help you build, launch, and execute an industry strategy or client experience plan that is right for you and your firm, so you can turbocharge growth and achieve extraordinary ROI for the investments you make in yourself, your professionals and your firm.

In the Appendixes that follow, I share a free guide called "Ten Steps to Executing the Successful Industry Strategy" that will get you started. When the time is right, reach out to me at Alice@LermanStrategies.com, and we'll have a no-obligation conversation.

Thanks again for reading Accountants! *Go Narrow*.

Appendix I
Ten Steps to Executing the Successful Industry Strategy

Firm Culture – Tactics for Change

1. **Industry Competency Framework (knowledge, skills and attributes expected for professionals at each level as they progress up the ladder)**

   - Integrated with current technical success factors
   - Map of preferred industry behaviors and activities at each level

2. **Industry Focus for All Firm Professionals**

   - Starting with the partner group
   - Supervisors and up should be expected to choose an industry focus.
   - Industry Major – primary focus / Minor – optional secondary focus

3. **Learning Opportunities Specific to Industry, Internal Communication and Knowledge Sharing**

   - Soft skills and technical skills to help associates move along the path to industry specialization

- Internal intranet portals in place and promoted by each industry team
- Improved information-sharing across all offices

Firm Growth Strategy – A Path to Success

4. Industry Leadership's Structural Hierarchy Elevates the Importance of Collaboration and Leveraging Industry Expertise Across the Firm

- Industry leadership reports on progress to the firm's executive leadership team.
- National industry leaders share best practices and consistency across industry practice groups.
- Dedicated marketing support is needed to support industry practices at both at the national and regional levels.

5. Formalized Industry Team Structure and Team Building

- National teams with representation from service lines and leaders of industry teams in the firm's offices or regions
- Primary responsibility of industry leadership teams: Strategic planning and collaboration
- Strategic partner and staffing needs should be identified to achieve goals in target markets and resource requisitions submitted.
- Acquisition targets should be identified to strengthen industries in key growth markets.

6. Annual Growth Goals and Accountability

- Each industry team to establish overall and specific service line growth goals.
    - Revenue goals should integrate into the regions' or offices' growth strategies.
- Industry marketplace goals should be established.
    - Conducting market-facing activities and producing industry thought leadership are the responsibilities of each industry group.
- Market-facing activities should be tracked and reported with an accountability tracker for each industry team's leaders and team members; the firm's management team can monitor action plans and behaviors.
    - Achievable goals will differ, based on level and career path.
    - Industry goals and progress measured against these goals should be integrated into the annual review process; the firm should require that industry goals and achievements are part of the goal setting and review process.

A Client Experience Strategy Intertwined with an Industry Strategy is the Key to Maximizing the Value of Both Investments to Achieve Accelerated and Sustainable Growth

7. "Voice of the client" feedback will help identify current strengths and weaknesses in how well clients are serviced today

- Each of the firm's industry practice groups and offices should launch and manage a consistent "voice of the client" feedback program
- Identifying quick wins to improve the current state of client experience and ensure that clients at risk are proactively managed and retained

8. Tiering the client portfolio helps shape and manage the investment in establishing a client experience model to optimize the value-added services provided to clients in each tier

9. Industry insights and expertise proactively offered as appropriate for each client tier will make the client experience strategy come to life

Required Systems to Support Industry Strategic Growth

10. Technology should automate and track industry and sector revenues

- NAICS code integration with billing system and/or CRM system
- Tracking of entity types to account for clients not easily defined by NAICS codes or those target markets that cut across industries, such as private equity groups, real estate investment trusts or funds, public company entities, nonprofit entities, government contractors and others
- Utilizing business intelligence tools to enhance industry financial dashboards
- A robust firm intranet platform will provide easy access to industry expertise and knowledge within the firm.
- Industry specialty/focus tracked on employee profiles and integrated with the firm's intranet search functionality
- Internal course offerings should be searchable by industry and sector.
- Industry revenue dashboards accessible to partners; these financial dashboards should offer partners national and regional financial reports so industry practice groups progress can be gauged.
- Industry financial reports should be available on a monthly, quarterly and annual basis; however, real-time live data-based industry reports are optimal.

Appendix II
A Phased Approach to Building an Industry Specialization Strategy

Execute the Industry Strategy in Phases

If your firm's industry strategy is starting at the ground floor, or your industry groups have a long way to go to become effective and productive, you can't get it all done at once! This process takes investments in time, changes in mindset, and it will not happen overnight. It makes sense to develop and execute an industry strategy in phases.

Phase I - Foundational

- Regional industry leaders, accountable to the regional managing partners (RMPs), and the office managing partners (OMPs) are responsible for collaborating with assurance, tax and consulting service line leaders to identify key markets and key sectors; create/maintain a cross-functional regional industry team; and to lead, coach and help local industry team members.
    - All three service lines should be represented on the team.
    - Establish a monthly meeting cadence, in-person when possible, or use video webcasts as necessary. At least one in-person meeting per year is recommended for each industry team.

- It's important to create momentum and consistency with meetings throughout the year, since each industry and service line will have differing busy seasons. Specific plans and tactics must be in place to execute year-round.
- Regional industry leaders are responsible for executing on the industry initiatives and delivering results in their local markets.
- RMPs/OMPs, assurance, tax, and consulting service line leaders are responsible for prioritizing resources, providing location and direction, and delivering results.

Phase II – Growth Culture and Industry Strategy

- Develop an industry growth strategy for the region, including go-to-market activities (in relevant industry associations, conferences, campaigns, webcasts, etc.), identification of fast-growth service lines, and pursuit plans for accounts and targets over $50K.
- The growth culture should be developed by working with RMPs/OMPs and assurance, tax and consulting service line leaders.
- Ensure professionals' self-selected industry majors and minors are vetted by location and used to assist with sales and marketing activities.
- Validate "qualified" prospects by location and determine whether pursuit teams are in place and active.
- Actively leverage rapid assessments (for accounts expected to generate fees over $50K), repeatable models,

and whiteboarding sessions; and spearhead rollout to gain introductions and demonstrate value.
- Create, maintain and lead industry teams, with an emphasis on growth in each geographic market.
- Review the written industry growth strategic plans to ensure consistency and ensure ideas are shared throughout the region.
- Senior managers, directors, and consulting managers (and selected tax and assurance managers) and above should participate on each market's industry teams.
- Interested supervisors and below should actively participate on industry growth teams. Supervisors can make a valuable contribution to industry teams by leveraging social media and by performing industry research and competitive intelligence.
- Work with a business development leader to determine if an industry-focused business developer is a good investment. If yes, recruit a business developer, approve his/her plan, and expect accountability for him/her to execute that business development plan, as part of the broader industry team's strategic growth plan.
- Work with RMPs and/or OMPs to determine involvement in pursuit opportunities over $50K (or the appropriate threshold for your firm). Involvement will vary based on the opportunity and may include input on service delivery team, scoping and presentations.
- RMPs, OMPs and tax and consulting service line leaders will assist by helping to create a culture that acknowledges that opportunities over $50K require the industry leader's involvement.

- Sales and marketing efforts are coordinated nationally, regionally and locally.
- Leverage marketing events (live or virtual), the firm's website, digital marketing campaigns, and thought leadership articles emailed to clients and prospects.
- Use marquee clients as references and gain testimonials with help from RMPs, OMPs and service line leaders.
- Promote the industry externally within the region.

Outcomes:

- The region significantly exceeds the profession's average growth rate.
- The region is achieving planned revenue dollars and year-over-year growth of XX% (consulting of xx%, tax of xx%, assurance of xx%).
- The industry practice is recognized as a leader in the market.

Regional Leader Role & Responsibilities

- Leads regional growth teams and coaches team members.
- Joins organizations and attends events.
- Develops new relationships and meets regularly with referral sources.
- Works with marketers to plan local/regional go-to-market activities and events.
- Attends all national industry team meetings and calls.

Industry Business Development and Marketing Meetings

WHO PARTICIPATES

Each region's or market's industry leader, marketing support lead, partners, business developers, and all other professionals in the market who want to benefit from and contribute to the work of the industry team.

WHAT HAPPENS

Effective business development requires frequent meetings (every two weeks at a minimum) to review target lists, cross-selling, and pipeline activities. The goal is to keep new business development top of mind and maintain proactive contacts with key targets.

Effectively building market reputation requires regular meetings (once a month at a minimum) to address market-facing activities such as firm-sponsored industry summits, networking events, articles for the national firm website, presentations, firm presence at industry associations, and encouraging individual networking and market-facing activities. The team collaborates to review ongoing activities in their region and how individuals are contributing to the groups' joint goals toward meeting their personal marketing plan and goals.

TOOLS REQUIRED

- Provide sample meeting agendas.
- Support each industry team with a personal

marketing plan template and an activity tracker, which helps hold team members accountable and aggregates activities of each market's team to become the joint activities across the entire national industry practice.
- Marketing assists in developing target lists for each partner (which should be captured in a shared CRM system).
- Use the firm's client database to gain a deep understanding of clients in each industry.

Phase III – Professional Development Focused on Building Industry Luminaries

- Develop an education plan, working with national industry leaders, firm learning experts and industry experts; and create a mechanism for delivering education throughout the region and/or nationally.
- Actively promote and deliver the education (regionally and locally) to develop industry experts (need to define and develop an approach to validate).
- Ensure managers and above have designated industry majors and minors.
- Ensure professionals with industry majors and minors are attending industry training and building expertise.
- Validate that industry majors and minors are, on an ongoing basis, reading thought leadership and information on emerging economic trends and are delivering knowledge to clients.
- Assist RMP/OMP/lines of business leaders with a talent plan to include resource needs, skills necessary,

levels, locations, and training.
- Assist in identifying and recruiting a key subject matter expert, working with the RMP, OMPs and service line leaders.
- Managers and above receive on average (over the course of three years), 10 hours of industry training per year, in their industry major. They are encouraged to "give back" to the firm by sharing their industry expertise internally, acting as industry course instructors as industry regulations, trends, and economic conditions change. This helps develop seasoned public speakers while helping everyone stay current and informed about their focus industry.
- Working with RMP/OMPs and service line leaders, determine the need for industry partners in each market and create a pipeline of partner candidates.

Outcomes

- A team of industry experts who deliver industry thought leadership to clients.
- Managers and above are deemed to be experts (internal validation process also needs to be established) in their selected majors.
- The marketplace recognizes the firm's industry expertise.

Appendix III
Sample Client Experience Standards, Based on Client/Prospect Tiers

Client/ Prospect Tier	Focused Program / Resources
Tier 1	- Industry "expert" involved in account - Participate in industry roundtables - Direct involvement in creating industry subject matter - Expertise in all service lines, as appropriate - Used as industry reference
Tier 2	- Industry subject matter expert visits - Industry thought leadership delivered - Team members involved in industry group - Participate in surveys/roundtables
Tier 3	- Exposure to industry expertise by all service lines - Delivery of specific thought leadership - Visit by regional industry champions - Participate in surveys
Tier 4	- Access to industry experts - Thought leadership delivered electronically - Local industry groups engaged

Glossary
Abbreviations and Acronyms

CRM – customer relationship management
CX – client experience
IMO – integrated marketing offering
KM – knowledge management
NAICS – North American Industry Classification System
OMP – office managing partner
RMP – regional managing partner

Acknowledgments

I'm forever grateful to the following leaders at accounting firms who inspired me to build my career, knowledge and skills around the concept of industry specialization as a path to career success and accounting firm financial success:

Ed Cary, who was National Industry Leader at Deloitte in the first decade of the 2000s;

Dorothy Alpert, who led the Real Estate National Industry practice at Deloitte in the 2000s;

Mendy Nudelman, who led the National Industry Program at RSM from 2011 through 2017;

Jay Weinstein, who has been the leader of growth and markets at EisnerAmper from early 2017;

Joe Natarelli, Lou Biscotti, and Matthew Bavolack, who are leaders, par excellence, of national industry practice groups at Marcum; and

Samantha Inczauskis, who enabled my success leading industries at RSM and Marcum, by managing all aspects of the firms' industry strategies operations at both RSM and Marcum.

About the Author

Over the last 18 years, Alice Lerman has developed a true passion for industry programs and for sharing her accumulated knowledge to help make professional services firms and individual professionals more successful. The reason is simple. As it turns out, accounting, tax and consulting service providers were way behind their clients. For years, their clients had been asking to be served by people who knew their businesses and their industries. They realized the importance of industry knowledge and experience in dealing with companies' most complex and difficult business issues. In other words: Accountants! *Go Narrow*.

Alice's "aha" moment came more than 16 years ago when she was working for a Big Four firm as a real estate industry knowledge manager. She moved through various industry-related roles focused on supporting the firm's real estate industry practice. As Alice progressed, she became an integral team contributor to the firm's developing industry specialization strategy. It opened her eyes to how a world-class enterprise focused on leveraging professionals across a wide array of functions, achieving extraordinary growth by building a reputation for deep expertise in its clients' industries.

Those years were her training ground before she founded her own consulting firm, Lerman Strategies. She learned how an industry strategy evolves and matures over time, how it intersects with other important firm-wide growth strategies, and how accountability, career incentives, rewards and recognitions, training, internal communications, change management and marketing strategies should all work together for the benefit of clients and the growth of the firm. More recently, Alice has led industry strategies at two of the nation's top 10 accounting firms and client experience strategies at two of the top 25 CPA firms.

Alice holds an MBA in Marketing and Management Strategies from Northwestern University, a law degree from Marquette University, and a Master's in Architecture and Urban Planning and a BA in History and Political Science, both from the University of Wisconsin-Milwaukee.

A mother of eight grown children, Alice lives in New Jersey with her husband, Jim, near many of their children and grandchildren. She's a world traveler who's more interested exploring the countryside than in touring the big cities.

www.lermanstrategies.com

Contact Alice: alice@lermanstrategies.com

www.LermanStrategies.com
Alice@LermanStrategies.com